Two Into One

A Comedy

Ray Cooney

A SAMUEL FRENCH ACTING EDITION

FOUNDED 1830

SAMUELFRENCH-LONDON.CO.UK
SAMUELFRENCH.COM

Cast in order of appearance

The Rt. Hon. Richard Willey MP	A smooth and rakishly handsome man in his mid-forties
Pamela Willey	A cosily attractive but impetuous woman
Receptionist	An efficient lady
Manager	A brusque man in his early sixties
Waiter	An Oriental, wily waiter
Lily Chatterton MP	A North-Country woman of about 50, with a forceful manner
George Pigden	A cheery man who is used to being put upon
Maria	A very pretty, young, Spanish chambermaid
Jennifer Bristow	A pretty, bright girl in her twenties
Edward	A tall, handsome young man in his twenties
Various Guests	

TWO INTO ONE

First performed at The Haymarket Theatre, Leicester, on 19th March, 1981, with the following cast of characters:

Pamela Willey	Jan Waters
Richard Willey	Richard Coleman
Chambermaid	Alexandra Chevitch
Waiter	Derek Royle
George Pigden	Ray Cooney
Manager	Anthony Sharp
Lily	Sheila Burrell
Jennifer Bristow	Debbi Blythe
Edward	Nick Field
Other Guests	James Williams, Harriet Ray, Kim Shadrake, Christopher Terry, Amanda Hendry

Directed by Roger Redfarn
Designed by Terry Parsons

The play was subsequently produced by The Theatre of Comedy Company on 19th October, 1984, at the Shaftesbury Theatre, London, with the following cast of characters:

Richard Willey	Donald Sinden
Pamela Willey	Barbara Murray
Receptionist	Ginni Barlow
Manager	Lionel Jeffries
Waiter	Derek Royle
Lily Chatterton	Jane Downs
George Pigden	Michael Williams
Maria	Carolyn Allen
Jennifer Bristow	Linda Hayden
Edward	Martin Connor
Hotel Guests	Christopher Chittell, Henry Tomlinson, Anthony Verner, Lorna Calleny, Maxine Daniels

Directed by Ray Cooney
Designed by Terry Parsons

The action of the play is continuous and takes place in the *Westminster Hotel*, London.

The set is a multiple one, utilizing a revolve and/or trucks. At various stages we see:

(a) The Lounge and Bedroom of Suite 648
(b) The Lounges of Suites 648 and 650
(c) The Lounge and Bedroom of Suite 650
(d) The main Hotel Reception area

Time—the present, a sunny day in early Spring

The Acting Edition is based on the production at the Shaftesbury Theatre, London, with sets, utilizing trucks, designed by Terry Parsons.

An alternative set design by Douglas Heap, which utilizes a revolve, is also available. For further details please apply to SIMPSON FOX ASSOCIATES, info@simpson-fox.com

Hotel Reception

Photograph by Donald Cooper

648 Bedroom and Lounge

ACT I

The main reception area of the Westminster Hotel. *A sunny day in early Spring*

The reception desk is C *with an arch in the rear leading off to an office area (unseen).* L *of the reception desk is a swing door leading to the hotel restaurant.* DL *are double lift doors.* R *of the reception desk is a phone kiosk. Right of the kiosk is the revolving door leading to the street. There is a table and chair* DLC *and another table with two chairs* DRC. *(Please see ground plan A on page 89)*

(NB. Throughout the two scenes in the reception area, hotel guests may be seen coming and going in the background providing they do not adversely affect either the action or the production budget)

When the CURTAIN *rises Pamela Willey is discovered seated at the table* DR *reading a magazine. Opposite her sits her husband, the Rt. Hon. Richard Willey M P. They make a very attractive couple and are both stylishly dressed. Richard exudes confidence and is a rakishly handsome man in his mid-forties. His tendency towards pomposity is (almost) totally offset by his charm. Pamela is a feminine, cosily attractive but impetuous woman who has subordinated her life to Richard's. Richard is looking a little impatient. Finally, he glances at his watch*

Richard Where the hell's the *coffee* got to?
Pamela *(after a pause)* It'll be along.
Richard I have a meeting at three o'clock.
Pamela *(still reading)* Mm?
Richard I'm due back at the Home Office at three.
Pamela Ah.
Richard We told that waiter at lunch we wanted coffee served out here.
Pamela Why not give it a miss if you're in a hurry.
Richard I want my coffee.
Pamela *(smiling)* Probably be drinking tea most of the afternoon, anyway.
Richard It's too bad, though. *(He moves to the reception desk)*
Pamela I don't think English was the waiter's strong subject.

Richard bangs the bell on the reception desk

Richard (*calling*) I say! (*To Pamela*) I ask you. Eighty-five pounds a day. And they weren't kidding when they said it excluded service.

Pamela Relax.

Richard Seriously, Pamela. You'd think the manager would have told the staff to look after me.

Pamela (*still reading*) Yes, dear.

Richard Must be good for business having Members of Parliament staying here.

Pamela I suppose they get rather blasé with all those foreign politicians coming over.

Richard (*edgily*) Darling, I'm the number two at the Home Office.

Pamela Yes. Do you think that explains the service we're getting?

Richard (*ignoring this; calling angrily*) Come on! (*He hits the bell*)

The female Receptionist appears

Receptionist You rang, Mr Willey?

Richard (*very smoothly*) Ah, yes. We asked for our coffee to be served out here.

Receptionist Oh, I'm sorry.

Richard (*smiling*) Quite all right. (*He indicates Pamela*) My wife was getting a trifle impatient, that's all.

Pamela gives him a look as the Receptionist comes out from behind the desk

Receptionist I'll see to it right away, Mr Willey.

Richard Thank you. I did ask the waiter while we were having lunch.

Receptionist I'll sort it out, sir.

The Receptionist exits into the restaurant

Richard (*returning to the table*) I suppose we should really move back to London and then we wouldn't have to suffer hotels at all.

Pamela Living in Sussex is very relaxing for you. All that beautiful fresh air and those lovely Downs. Keeps you in touch with your constituents, too. You've always said how important that is.

Richard I know but there are periods when I'm up to my eyes. Like now, with this Vice Bill. Committee meetings, delegations, conferences. When it comes to pornography everybody wants to take up a position.

Pamela (*laughing*) Very good, Richard!

Richard looks blank

Richard What with the Home Secretary on one hand, the Police Federation on the other and the Prime Minister sticking her oar in every five minutes——

Pamela So when it gets as hectic as this we stay here. And whatever you say about the *Westminster Hotel*, it's handy for the Home Office, for Downing Street and for the House of Commons.

Richard (*grudgingly*) Well . . .

Pamela Makes a pleasant break for me, too. Three or four times a year. Bit of shopping. See the matinée of a play. I only wish I could persuade you to take it easy once in a while.

The Receptionist returns from the restaurant

Receptionist Coffee on its way, Mr Willey.

Richard Ah. (*To Pamela*) Told you it would be all right. (*To the Receptionist*) Thank you very much. (*He smiles at her*)

The Receptionist returns to the reception desk and exits into the rear

Pamela (*after a pause, conversationally*) Let's spend the afternoon upstairs in bed.

Richard slowly looks at her in amazement

Richard Pamela! I have to meet a delegation comprised of the Police Commissioner, the Attorney General and the Chairman of the TUC.

Pamela I don't think I can cope with them as well.

Richard gives her a surprised look

Richard I knew you should never have had that glass of wine with your lunch.

Pamela I think it's something to do with staying in hotels. Especially midweek. Go on. Let someone else handle the meeting this afternoon.

Richard It's impossible.

Pamela We *used* to go to bed in the afternoons. Or sometimes just lay out in front of the fire.

Richard Pamela, we've been married eighteen years on the twenty-fifth of June.

Pamela Nobody told me it was all going to stop on an exact date.

Richard It *hasn't* all stopped.

Pamela Petering out a bit though, isn't it?

Richard Did you have oysters for lunch?

Pamela I'm only saying that you should try and relax a bit more. That *we* should try and relax. Together. The PM's very sensible about that. She's very good at relaxing.

Richard I'm damn sure she and Dennis don't stretch out on the carpet every afternoon.

Pamela (*thoughtfully*) I don't know. The way her hair always looks so flat at the back makes me suspicious.

Richard looks perplexed at this example of feminine logic and then glances at his watch again

Just skip the coffee, darling.

Richard No, I've got to wait for Pigden anyway.

Pamela (*pleasantly surprised*) You didn't say George was coming over.

Richard He's calling in with my papers.

Pamela Ah! Dear George.

Richard Not a bad sort for a civil servant.

Pamela He's a bit reserved, that's all. Only needs the right person to grab hold of him, give him a kiss and a cuddle.

Richard Well, I don't think that's on our agenda this afternoon.

The Chinese Waiter enters from the restaurant and looks around

Ah! Thank you.

The Waiter goes over to them and takes out his pad

Waiter Yes, sir.

Richard Where's our coffee?

Waiter Coffee? You no want lunch first?

Richard We've *had* lunch!

Waiter (*blankly*) You've had lunch.

Pamela Mr and Mrs Willey. Suite six-four-eight.

The Waiter looks through his pad

Richard And we ordered coffee in the restaurant.

Waiter No Willey, no six-four-eight.

Richard And we asked your receptionist, too. So this makes three times.

Waiter (*writing*) Three times.

Richard Are you by any chance the same waiter who served us breakfast in our room this morning?

Waiter Yes, thank you, room service.

Richard That explains a lot.

Waiter Mistake with breakfast?

Pamela (*quickly*) It was delicious.

Richard Except that if you order continental breakfast you don't expect lamb chops, sausage, bacon, eggs and tomato.

Waiter (*writing*) You want lamb chops, sausage——

Richard God!

Pamela No! Just coffee!

The Waiter exits into the restaurant as Lily Chatterton enters from the restaurant. She is a forceful, North-Country MP in her fifties

Lily Richard Willey!

Richard (*seeing Lily; quietly*) Oh, my God! (*To Lily, brightly*) Hello, Lily.

Lily Fancy bumping into you. And it's Mrs Willey, isn't it?

Pamela (*not recognizing Lily*) Yes, that's right.

Lily Lily Chatterton.

Pamela Of course! You're a friend of Richard's.

Lily Am I hell, I'm a Labour MP.

Richard Lily represents Bradford East.

Lily You two aren't stopping here, are you?

Richard Couple of days.

Lily Well, that's a turn up for the book. Since when have Conservative ministers stayed in hotels with their *wives*?

Pamela laughs. Richard manages a smile

Richard I'm only a junior minister remember.
Lily Of course. (*To Pamela*) Plenty of time for the lad to develop bad habits.
Pamela Are you staying here, Mrs Chatterton?
Lily Only 'til tomorrow. It'll be a late session in the Commons tonight. Very important Bill being discussed, eh Richard?
Richard Very. (*To Pamela*) It's Lily's favourite thing. Vice.
Lily (*to Pamela*) Pornography and corruption actually. (*Strongly*) This government is so wishy-washy I've had to put it through as a Private Member's Bill. (*To Richard*) I hope you've done your homework, that's all.
Richard I can assure you I'm extremely well briefed.
Lily Well, I've subjected myself personally to eighteen and a half hours of perverted sex.

Richard tries not to smile

Pamela (*at a loss*) Seems rather a lot.
Lily Mrs Willey, you wouldn't believe some of those video films. Filthy! I couldn't understand half the things they were doing first time through.

Richards gives a polite smile

Pamela I'm sure both the Home Secretary and Richard are as concerned as anyone.

Richard sneezes

Lily Bless you.
Richard Blasted hay fever.
Pamela Oh no! When did that start?
Richard This morning.
Pamela Well, I'm pretty sure I packed your anti-histamine tablets.
Richard Damn nuisance.
Lily (*to Pamela*) My husband's a sufferer, you know.
Richard I can imagine!

The Waiter enters with a large tray on which are three pots of coffee, six cups and saucers and six milk jugs. He puts the tray down on Richard's table

Waiter Three pot coffee.

Richard and Pamela react

Pamela Er—no. I think there's been a mistake.
Waiter (*referring to his pad*) Willey. Suite six-four-eight.
Pamela Yes. But we ordered only one pot.
Waiter (*referring to his pad*) No. Most definite. Two coffees, two persons— three times. (*He indicates*) Three pots, six cups.
Richard *Two* coffees.
Waiter You want two more?
Richard God!
Pamela That's quite enough, thank you.

The Waiter exits

Lily Usual Home Office cock up! I'll leave you then, Mrs Willey. (*She starts to move towards the lifts*)
Pamela You MPs never stop working.
Lily Oh, I'm not working, I'm having a nice relaxing afternoon getting ready for the fray tonight.
Pamela I wish someone could persuade Richard to relax once in a while.
Lily He couldn't do that. He'd get a little smack from Mrs Thatcher. I'll talk to you later, Mrs Willey. What room are you in?
Pamela Six-four-eight.
Lily Oh, *I'm* on the sixth floor, too. I'll see you both around. (*She moves away towards lift and presses the button*)
Richard (*quietly to Pamela*) Not if I can help it.

Lily gets into the lift and departs as the Manager comes out of the restaurant

Manager Ah, you've been attended to, Mr Willey?
Richard Yes, thank you. We've got coffee for Africa.

The Manager looks blank for a moment

Manager Splendid.

Richard reacts to the Manager's indifference

The Manager goes to the reception desk and exits into the rear office

Richard What are your plans this afternoon, darling?
Pamela I've told you. I'm seeing the matinée of *Evita*.
Richard God, that's been on for years. You'd think after the Falklands crisis that the public would resent paying ten pounds a head to be told "Don't cry for me Argentina". God! Three pots, six cups and no sugar! (*He strides towards the restaurant*)
Pamela For God's sake, don't call him back!

George Pigden enters through the revolving door carrying his briefcase (on which are his initials "GP") a rolled umbrella and wearing a bowler hat. He is a cheery man who is used to being put upon

George Ah, there you are, Mr Willey.
Richard George! About time too.
George I'm not late, am I? (*He looks at his watch*) One forty-five.
Pamela Course you're not late, George. You're never late.
George (*seeing Pamela*) Oh. (*Smiling*) Good-afternoon, Mrs Willey.
Pamela Good-afternoon, George. You're looking dapper as usual. A very spruce personal private secretary.
George (*pleased*) Thank you. I try to look smart for the office.
Richard You look like an undertaker.
George Oh, Mr Willey! (*He emits a foolish chuckle*)
Pamela No, you don't, George. Mr Willey's in a bad mood. Coffee, George?

George No, thank you. (*He sees the coffee*) I say, what have you had? A coffee morning? (*He chuckles at his little joke*)

Richard Have you noticed, Pamela, that George is always so damned cheerful?

Pamela (*smiling at George*) Yes, I have.

George We have to keep smiling, Mr Willey.

Richard Do we really?

George That's what the Home Secretary says.

Richard Yes, well the Home Secretary doesn't have his coffee at the *Westminster Hotel*. Got my papers?

George Oh yes. All the nitty gritty there for this afternoon. (*He indicates his briefcase*)

Richard takes George's hat and umbrella and puts them on the table DR

Richard Pull up a chair, George.

Pamela (*taking the room key from her handbag*) Well, if you're going to discuss parliamentary business I shall go and make myself look beautiful.

George (*gallantly*) That won't take very long, Mrs Willey.

Pamela turns and looks pleased. Richard gives George a withering glance. George happily smiles

Richard (*to George, coldly*) Are you hoping for a *long* career at the Home Office?

Pamela That was a very sweet remark, George. Maybe Richard could take a few tips from you on how to win over the female voter. (*She surreptitiously pats Richard's leg*)

During the next two speeches Pamela gets into one of the lifts and departs

Richard Right, George. What's on the agenda for this afternoon?

George sits at the DR *table, puts his briefcase on the floor and refers to his papers*

George Well, it's all very informal, really. Reception's at three o'clock. The delegates will have had a working lunch to thrash out any problems. The Home Secretary has attached his notes to your report, Mr Willey.

Pamela has departed. Richard pulls George downstage C

Richard Right. Stop prattling on. Let's get down to business, George.

George Business? I thought that's what we *were* doing.

Richard (*pressing on*) I want you to do me a little favour.

George Naturally, if it's within——

Richard It is. I want you to book me another room here.

George What's wrong with your suite?

Richard Nothing, it's fine.

George Why do you want to move then?

Richard I don't! I want *another* room. From two-thirty until five p.m.

George Something to do with your wife?

Richard No. Something to do with my girl-friend.

George (*blankly*) Your girl-friend? (*Realizing*) Oh, Mr Willey!

Richard You're not going to burst into song, are you?

George You should think of your position.

Richard (*sexily*) Oh, I am, George, I am.

George But why *here*? In the *Westminster Hotel*?

Richard That's what's so perfect. I'm staying here anyway. Much safer than us going to some other hotel where I might be recognized.

George But you've got that delegation at the Home Office this afternoon.

Richard There's half a dozen people in the department who can supervise that. Tell Mr Doubleday to take the chair. He'll be tickled pink. Say I've been called back to Worthing on urgent constituency business.

George Mr Willey, if the Home Secretary were to discover——

Richard George, the Home Secretary has only just discovered that the Conservatives won the last General Election.

Richard sits George at the DR *table*

George It's all so dangerous.

Richard I know. That's half the attraction. It'll be dead easy, George. You just go to the reception there and book a double room.

George Why *me*?

Richard Well, *I* can't do it, can I! Now you simply check in as Sir Charles Easter——

George *Who*?

Richard Sir Charles Easter.

George Oh, my goodness.

Richard The more impressive you sound, the fewer questions they ask.

George I'm not practised in this kind of thing.

Richard (*sitting at the* DR *table*) Well, now's your chance to learn. Explain you want a nice double room for about two and a half hours while you and Lady Easter——

George Oh, God!

Richard (*pressing on*) While you and Lady Easter are passing through London. You live in the country—Chichester or somewhere.

George holds his head in his hands

(*Pouring George a cup of coffee*) You've dropped Lady Easter off at the hairdressers while you check in and—er—she'll be joining you in your room later. It's a piece of cake.

George Why can't your lady friend just come in and book the room?

Richard Not a good idea, George.

George Why not?

Richard Too many politicians knocking about the place. She might be recognized.

George (*worried*) Recognized?

Richard Don't worry, it's not Mrs Thatcher.

George I suppose we should be grateful for small mercies.

Richard It's one of her secretaries, actually.

George What?

Richard One of the PM's secretaries. Jennifer Bristow.
George (*wide-eyed*) Jennifer Bristow?
Richard Have you noticed her?
George You can't miss her!
Richard Gorgeous, isn't she?
George She's married!
Richard And that's just *one* of the plusses, George.
George (*pleading*) No, no—please. There've been enough scandals. The
   Opposition is just waiting to put the boot in. (*Aghast*) There's this new
   Vice Bill—the debate on pornography. They'd have a field day.
Richard Nothing can go wrong.
George That's what Chamberlain said at Munich. Mr Willey, think of the
   Party.
Richard All I can think of at the moment is Mrs Bristow. I've been waiting
   for weeks, George. We won't get another opportunity like this.
George You mean you haven't yet actually . . .
Richard No, I haven't yet actually and it's driving me insane.
George Well, all I can say is Mrs Thatcher wouldn't like it.
Richard There's an answer to that, George.

The Waiter enters from the restaurant with six sugar bowls on a tray

Waiter Me forgot sugar.
Richard Go away!

The Waiter exits, chuckling to himself

   Right now, listen. Here's Mrs Bristow's home telephone number. (*He
   hands George a piece of paper. Grinning*) She's taken a day's sick leave.
   She's waiting at her flat for you to ring and tell her the number of the
   hotel room.
George (*annoyed*) Oh, is she?
Richard She'll be over here in five minutes. They only live in Sloane Square.
George (*rising and breaking away*) Well, I don't think that either you or Mrs
   Bristow should have taken me for granted. I don't approve and you know
   it. I just keep thinking of your wife all the time.
Richard OK, that's a fair swap. Oh, come on, George. (*Wheedling*) Your
   minister *needs* you.

George doesn't weaken

   George, if ever you get married I'll do the same for you.

George glares at him

   George. George Pigden—OBE.
George Don't try and bribe me!
Richard (*rising*) Well, do as you're bloody well told then! (*Quickly*) I'm
   sorry, George. God, I'm *sorry*. You can see I'm desperate for the girl.
George (*weakening*) I just wish I could persuade you to change your mind.
Richard Could they have persuaded Nelson to give up Lady Hamilton?

George And look what happened to him. Finished up with one arm and his eye in a sling.

Richard tries to work this out

Richard Please, George!
George Oh, very well!
Richard Good man! Oh, by the way, you don't have to worry about Mrs Bristow's husband.
George (*nervously*) Why, what does he do?
Richard God knows what he does but he's not around at the moment—that's the main thing. Jennifer's a clever girl. She's packed him off on a skiing holiday.
George Skiing holiday?
Richard The Italian Alps. You see, George. Everybody's getting treats. Now don't forget to ring her and don't forget to bring me the key——

Pamela alights from the lift. She is now wearing her jacket

(*Seeing Pamela, indicating to George that she is there*)—the *key* to this debate, George, is the support of the backbenchers, and the *key* to their support ... (*He feigns seeing her*) Hello, darling! You look fantastic. Doesn't she look fantastic, George? Fantastic, Pamela.
Pamela Amazing what a jacket can do.
Richard But what a jacket! (*Brightly*) You know, George, it wouldn't surprise me if Mrs Willey weren't going to see *Evita* at all. While I'm slaving away over this vice bill, she'll be upstairs in our room locked in the arms of a man. What do you think, George?

George hesitates and then emits his foolish chuckle as though in response to Richard's kidding

No! (*He hugs Pamela*) I'm only joking, darling. You're as trustworthy as an old pit pony.

Pamela gives him an icy look

Pamela (*angrily*) For all you know I could be having dozens of affairs. I might be sleeping with George twice a week.
George (*giggling nervously*) Steady on!
Richard (*chuckling*) You and George?
Pamela You don't think I'm prone to it.
Richard No, I don't. I don't think he's up to it either.
George Thank you.
Pamela (*to Richard*) Just you stop getting at George. I'm sure he's got a dozen girl-friends.
Richard (*chuckling*) Chance would be a fine thing, eh, George?
George Well, living at home with Mother does make for difficulties. She's a bit old-fashioned, you know.
Pamela Well if it's opportunity that's missing, George, what are you up to this afternoon?
George This afternoon?

Pamela Why not do something really romantic. Ask one of your nice little secretaries to come and spend the afternoon with you in our suite.

George looks blank for a moment and then looks at Richard who gives him a quick humourless smile. George then looks back at Pamela and once more emits his nervous chuckle

George (*foolishly*) I couldn't do that.
Richard Certainly not.
Pamela You're at the Home Office. I'm at the theatre. (*To George*) Be our guest.
Richard I don't know what's got into you this afternoon, Pamela. Finish your coffee, George, while I see Mrs Willey into a taxi.
Pamela (*surprised*) Thank you, darling.
Richard Then I'll stroll round the corner to the Home Office.
Pamela Well, don't overdo it this afternoon.
Richard I'll try not to. Bye then, George.
Pamela Bye, George.

Pamela and Richard go out through the revolving door

George worried, collects his briefcase, hat and umbrella and moves to the desk

Richard returns

Richard (*hastily to George*) Soon as you've checked in, ring Mrs Bristow with the room number. I'll walk round the block and meet you back here for the key. Remember, Sir Charles *Easter*!

Pamela returns

Pamela Come on, Richard.
Richard (*briskly*) Easter, yes. Happy Easter, George!
Pamela Easter?
Richard Give a week or two.

Richard exits through the revolving door

Pamela If you change your mind about one of your secretaries ...
George No, I can't!

Richard re-appears

Richard Come on, Pamela. Taxi.
Pamela (*as she goes*) Bye, George!
Richard (*as he goes*) Bye, George!
George (*confused*) Bye, George! (*He stands L of the desk*)

Richard and Pamela exit via the revolving door

The Waiter, unseen by George, enters to clear Richard's coffee things. He stands beside George

Waiter Excuse, please.
George (*jumping*) Easter! Oh. Give a week or two.

Waiter (*blankly*) Thank you. Finish coffee?
George Yes. Thank you, finish coffee.

The Waiter collects the tray

Waiter All three pot?
George Three pot, yes.
Waiter (*chuckling*) Three pot potty.

The Waiter takes the tray towards the restaurant. George hits the bell on reception desk

(*Turning*) You want more coffee?
George No, thank you.

The Waiter shrugs and exits

George hesitates and then puts his hat, umbrella and briefcase on the desk. After a moment's pause he hits the bell again and then looks around apprehensively

The Receptionist appears from the office

George, not realizing that she has arrived, turns and hits the bell. he then reacts as he sees her standing next to him behind the desk

Receptionist Sorry to have kept you, sir.
George (*with furtive nonchalance*) Oh, fine! That's all right. I—er—I want to book a nice double hotel, please. Room! I'd like a double, please. A double room.
Receptionist (*pleasantly, but apprehensively*) Double room. When for, sir?
George I'd like to start in about five minutes.

The Receptionist is getting wary

Receptionist You'd like to check in *now*.
George Yes, please.
Receptionist And for how many nights?
George Two and a half hours.
Receptionist Two and a half hours?
George Yes. (*He plunges in*) My wife and I are just passing through—er—through London. Yes. My wife and I have travelled over from—er—Norfolk, Norfolk, yes—we're just up from the Downs. And my wife and I are driving down to—er—Devon. Yes. Glorious—er—Devon—and we're going via Staines and—Chipping Sodbury. And I've dropped my wife somewhere—er—at the hairdressers. Yes, she's gone to the hair-dressers to—have her hair done. So I'm checking in and as soon as my wife has had her hair done, she'll arrive here—and we'll go straight to bed.
Receptionist (*after a pause*) If you wait here, I'll get the manager.

The Receptionist exits into the rear of the reception area

George looks around nervously

The Manager enters and coughs to attract George's attention

George jumps and accidentally hits the bell with his elbow

Manager I gather you want a double room for the afternoon, sir.

George (*broadly*) Yes, that's about it. My wife and I are up from Norfolk. On our way to Devon. Staines. Chipping er—she's been dropped—my wife has. I've dropped her at the—er—er. . .

Manager (*impassively*) The hairdressers?

George Thank you, yes. I'm checking in and as soon as my wife arrives, she'll be whacked—we both will be. So we're going straight to bed. (*He tries to smile nonchalantly at the Manager*) For about two and a half hours.

Manager Yes, I see. Well, that's fine. If I could just have your name. (*He prepares to write in the register*)

George My name. Why not.

Pamela is seen returning through the revolving door

(*Seeing Pamela*) Christmas! (*He picks up the* Daily Telegraph *and opens it in front of his face to mask himself from Pamela. He steps back into the corner between the desk and the restaurant swing door*)

Manager Christmas. Is that C-H-R-I . . .?

The Manager looks up and is surprised to see George deep in the newspaper, tucked away in the corner. Pamela has reached R of the desk

Pamela Six-four-eight, please.

Manager (*getting the key*) Certainly, Mrs Willey.

Pamela My taxi got half way to the theatre before I realized I'd left my theatre ticket upstairs.

Manager Oh, dear.

He gives her the key. She hurries towards the lifts and presses the lift button

(*To George*) How do you spell Christmas, sir?

There is no answer from George who is still behind the newspaper

Excuse me, sir.

Pamela gets into the lift and departs

George's head appears from behind paper. He checks that Pamela has gone and then looks at the Manager

George Yes?

Manager How do you spell Christmas, Mr Christmas?

George (*bemused*) Mr Christmas?

Manager As in Noel?

George What. Oh yes. That's it. Noel. That's my name—Noel.

Manager (*surprised*) Noel Christmas.

George (*blankly*) Noel Christmas. (*To the Manager*) Unusual, isn't it?

Manager Yes. (*Writing*) Noel Christmas.

George Now, could we be very quick please. I am most anxious to get upstairs with my wife.

Manager Yes. As soon as you've registered, sir.

George I have registered. Noel Christmas.

Manager (*preparing to write*) And your address? (*He waits*)

George Norfolk.

Manager Norfolk?

George That'll find me. I'm very big on the Broads. (*He looks anxiously towards the lifts in case Pamela should return*)

Manager I'm sorry to be difficult, sir. I need your full address.

George Number twenty-four.

Manager (*writing*) Twenty-four. (*He looks up at George*)

George The High Street.

Manager (*writing*) The High Street. (*He looks up at George*)

George Norfolk.

Manager (*controlling himself*) Whereabouts in Norfolk?

George Chichester.

Manager (*giving George a deadpan look*) I thought Chichester was in Sussex.

George Just testing you. (*He chuckles*) How about Norwich?

Manager To the best of my recollection, Norwich *is* in Norfolk.

George (*congratulatory*) Very good! Twenty-four The High Street, Norwich.

Manager If you'd just sign the register.

George Certainly.

Manager I'll get your key.

George Thank you. (*Signing with a flourish*) Noel Christmas.

The Manager gives him the key

Thank you most kindly. (*He puts the key in his pocket and picks up his hat and umbrella*)

Manager I'll have you shown to your suite.

George Don't bother. I'll find the way. (*He hurries towards the lifts*)

Manager Excuse me, sir!

George Yes?

Manager Is this your briefcase?

George Oh, yes. Thank you. (*He goes back to the desk*)

Manager Ah, no sorry, sir. It's somebody else's.

George No, that's mine.

Manager I think not. (*He points to the initials*) GP.

George Yes.

Manager Yours would be NC.

George NC?

Manager Noel Christmas.

George Ah—yes! GP. Didn't I tell you? I'm the local doctor. (*He takes the briefcase*)

Manager (*nonplussed*) Doctor?

George Yes. (*Pointing to the initials*) General Practitioner. Dr Christmas of Norwich. (*He moves to the lifts*)

Pamela and Lily step out from one of the lifts engrossed in conversation

George, in his panic, throws the briefcase in the air and puts the Daily Telegraph *in front of his face once more*

The surprised Waiter enters from the restaurant to find that the briefcase drops into his arms

The Manager reacts to all this but the two women are oblivious. George grabs the briefcase from a bemused Waiter and pushes him off with the umbrella and hat into the restaurant

The Waiter exits

George sits at the DL *table with his head buried in the* Daily Telegraph

Lily (*entering from the lift*) And the Home Secretary's record is just not good enough, Mrs Willey.

Pamela Well, I don't think we can blame the Home Secretary for all the vice clubs in Soho.

Lily Too many police, my dear. I'll see you later. Maybe we can have a cup of tea or something.

Lily exits through the revolving door

Pamela (*holding up the envelope; to the Manager*) I found it.

Manager (*riveted by George*) I beg your pardon, Mrs Willey?

Pamela My theatre ticket. I found it.

Manager Oh, good.

Pamela Oh! Do you have the telephone number of the Prince Edward Theatre by any chance?

Manager Prince Edward Theatre.

Pamela Where *Evita* is playing. I'd like to know what time the matinée starts. It's either two-thirty or three.

Manager That'll be in the entertainment guide of the morning paper. (*Calling to George*) Excuse me, sir.

George wraps the paper further round his face. Pamela and the Manager exchange a glance

May we borrow the newspaper, please, sir?

George sinks lower in the chair and opens the newspaper wide in front of his face to mask him from Pamela

Pamela (*moving towards George*) I won't keep it a moment.

There is a pause and then George hands over all the Telegraph *except the front and back page. The Manager comes from behind the desk and joins Pamela*

Manager Madam would like to glance at the theatre guide if you don't mind, sir.

George tears the front page from the back page and hands the front page over to Pamela whilst still covering his face with the back page

The theatre guide is on the inside of the back page.

After a pause George speaks from behind the newspaper, using a disguised adenoidal voice

George *Evita* matinée, three o'clock.

Pamela and the Manager exchange a glance

Pamela Thank you. Does it say what time it finishes?
George (*still with a nasal voice*) No, it doesn't.
Manager (*to Pamela*) The box office will be able to tell you. (*To George*) Is there a number?
George (*with a nasal voice*) Box office four-three-seven six-eight-seven-seven.

Slowly the top of the newspaper flops over revealing George's face. George is oblivious because he is reading

Credit cards are available on o-one–four-three-seven six-eight-seven-eight. Group bookings are available on o-one–eight-three-nine three-o-nine-two.

George realizes that Pamela is staring at him

(*Still in a nasal voice*) Would you like to know about any other ... (*He stops and reverts to his normal voice*) Would you like to know about any other shows?
Pamela (*dumbly*) No thank you.

The Manager has written the number on a piece of paper

Manager Four-three-seven six-eight-seven-seven was that, sir?
George (*still nasal*) Yes, six-eight-seven-seven. I mean—(*correctly*)—six-eight-seven-seven. (*He pretends to nonchalantly read the page of his paper*)
Manager You can use the phone over there, Mrs Willey.

Pamela is staring at George

Mrs Willey—phone over there. (*He indicates the phone kiosk and takes the newspaper from her*)
Pamela (*still looking at George*) Thank you. (*She starts to move*)
Manager (*to George*) Is there anything I can do for you, Dr Christmas?

George's newspaper falls. Pamela stops and slowly turns

George (*faintly*) No.
Manager And you'll be joined later in your room by *Mrs* Christmas?

George's face crumbles as Pamela reacts to "Mrs Christmas". Pamela grins broadly

George (*faintly*) Yes.

Manager Fine.

The Manager exits into the rear of the reception area

George (*pulling Pamela away*) I can explain everything.
Pamela (*delighted*) You don't have to. You changed your mind about a naughty afternoon.
George (*bewildered*) Did I?
Pamela But you've booked into some other room.

George hesitates

George (*foolishly giggling*) Yes.
Pamela Thought it was a bit off to use ours, did you?
George (*foolishly giggling*) Yes.
Pamela (*laughing*) And what's that you're calling yourself?
George (*foolishly giggling*) Dr Christmas.
Pamela I knew there was more to you than meets the eye.
George (*foolishly giggling*) Yes.
Pamela So who's the lucky girl then?
George What lucky girl?
Pamela The one you're spending the afternoon with!

Richard is seen entering from the revolving door

George (*quickly*) You!
Pamela What?
George It's you!

George still clutching his briefcase, in his panic embraces Pamela and bundles her into a lift and hits the button. As the lift door closes George gives the staggered Pamela a huge kiss to prevent her seeing Richard

Richard hurries over to the desk and hits the bell, not having seen any of the foregoing

The Receptionist appears, followed by the Manager. The Manager puts the mail in the rack

Receptionist Yes, Mr Willey?
Richard Ah. (*Broadly*) I've—er—I've been expecting an *old friend* of mine to arrive. Sir Charles Easter.
Receptionist (*looking through the register*) Sir Charles Easter.

Richard smiles happily as he waits. He sneezes

Manager (*looking up*) Bless you!
Richard Thank you. Lovely fellow, Charlie. Just like to say hello.
Receptionist No, sir.
Richard (*surprised*) What?
Receptionist Only three arrivals this morning and no-one by the name of Easter.
Richard Bloody fool!
Manager (*looking up*) I beg your pardon, sir!

Richard Not you. My friend Easter. I'd better make a phone call. (*He moves to the revolving door*)
Receptionist Public phone booth just there, sir.
Richard No, I think I'll use the one round the corner!

Richards exits by the revolving door as the Manager exits into the rear of reception

The lift door opens. George comes out wildly looking around for Richard. Pamela comes out in a trance

Pamela (*entering*) Could any of the staff use a ticket for this afternoon's matinée of *Evita*? (*She reaches the desk*)
Receptionist Oh. I'll go and ask. Thank you, Mrs Willey.

The Receptionist takes the envelope from Pamela and exits into the rear

George Mrs Willey——
Pamela (*sexily*) Just call me Mrs Christmas.
George No, you see about my behaviour just now——
Pamela Tell me about it upstairs, George.
George Well, you probably want time——
Pamela No, I don't, George. I know what I'm doing.
George Thank God one of us does.
Pamela This is how it should be. Foolish. Impetuous!
George But not suicidal.
Pamela Tell you what. I'll go upstairs and get out a very naughty nightie— just for you.
George No, I never wear them. (*Realizing*) Oh. No, I wouldn't bother——

The Manager enters from the rear of reception

Pamela I won't be long, George. (*For the Manager's benefit*) Most pleasant to have met you, Dr Christmas! Enjoy your stay in London, Doctor!

Pamela goes into one of the lifts and departs

George Wait a minute, there'll be a ghastly ...

She has gone

Manager Something wrong, Doctor?
George No. No. Everything in the rosy is garden. (*He takes the key from his pocket*)
Manager Yes. Well, we'll have your wife shown up to your room when she arrives.
George Yes. No! I'd forgotten about her. She doesn't like to be shown up. She'll come straight to the room. She won't stop and say hello to you or anything like that. Straight in, straight up, straight into bed. She's very— er ... (*he mimes "sexy"*) only with me, of course. She doesn't like anybody else. Doesn't want to meet anybody else. Agoraphobia. Fear of meeting people. Yes. She's been under me for years. Yes, well, I'll go up to my room—(*Suddenly seeing the number on his key, yelling*) Ah!

Manager What on earth . . .?
George I'd like to change my room, please.
Manager Change it? You haven't seen it yet, have you?
George No, I don't want to see it either. It's the number.

George shows the Manager the number. The Manager takes the key

Manager What's the matter with the number?
George Six-fifty.
Manager That's right. Suite six-fifty. What's wrong with it?
George Six-fifty is near to six-four-eight, isn't it?
Manager It's next to it.
George That's what's wrong with it. Mr Willey's in six-four-eight.
Manager Ye-es.
George Too close.
Manager Who's too close?
George Mr Willey—to me. I can't have it.
Manager You know Mr Willey, do you?

George goes to say "yes" but stops

George No, I don't! I don't want to know him either. He's in the
Government, isn't he?
Manager Ye-es.
George I refuse to be in the next room to a man who hobnobs with Robin
Day and appears on *Panorama*.
Manager I'm afraid we have no other room, Doctor. Now whatever your
views on Mr Willey's politics, I must ask you not to impinge upon his
privacy whilst you're in my hotel.

*The Manager hands back the key to George and exits into the restaurant.
Richard enters through the revolving door*

Richard George, where have you been?
George (*going to Richard*) Thank heavens! (*He pulls him downstage*)
Richard Jennifer's number's permanently engaged. Have you been phoning
her?
George No, I haven't.
Richard You booked the room though, didn't you?
George Yes, but it's six-fifty!
Richard Very cheap, how did you manage that?
George The number—six-fifty.
Richard Oh well, can't be helped.
George Please, Mr Willey. The whole thing must be called off. For
everybody's sake.
Richard What's the matter, George! You've done very well so far.
George No, I haven't! Please! Go back to the Home Office. We'll *both* go
back to the Home Office.
Richard Don't be ridiculous! Get yourself into suite six-fifty and order some
champagne and smoked salmon sandwiches.
George I couldn't eat a thing, honestly.

Richard Not for you!

The Manager enters from the restaurant and moves towards the desk

George Mr Willey, you have no idea where this will end.
Richard Oh, yes I have!
George It will be total disarray.
Manager (*joining them*) Is something wrong, Mr Willey?
Richard No, no, no. I'm just so thrilled to see him. (*Hugging George*) This is my old chum I've been waiting for.
Manager (*surprised*) Is it?
Richard It most certainly is.
George I'm afraid it isn't.
Richard It isn't?
George No.
Richard Oh.
George That's what I was trying to explain. We've never met.
Richard We haven't?
George No. (*To the Manager*) I was telling you that, wasn't I? Just now.

The Manager nods dumbly

Richard Oh. So you're not Charlie Easter from Chichester?
George No, I'm Noel Christmas from Norwich.

Richard closes his eyes in anguish. George tries to smile

I thought you'd be surprised.
Richard I'm amazed! (*To the Manager*) He's the spitting image of Sir Charles Easter!
Manager (*blankly*) Is he?
Richard Yes. (*To George, at a loss*) Noel Christmas, you say?
George Yes. (*Pointedly*) And I was telling the manager I'm most concerned he's put *Christmas* right next door to *Willey*!
Manager (*to Richard*) He appears to have a thing about politicians.
Richard Probably patted too hard on the head when he was a baby. (*To George*) Nice to have chatted to you, sir. I'll see you around on the sixth floor.

Richard pushes George off towards the lift

(*To the Manager*) Nothing like Charlie from the rear.
Manager Just ring reception if he attempts to interfere with you again, Mr Willey. We'll put Security on to it.
Richard Thank you. Excuse me, I need to make a phone call.

Richard goes to move to the phone kiosk as George stops just as he is about to get into the lift

George Ah!

Richard and the Manager stop and turn. George hurries back to them

(*To Richard*) I forgot!

Richard What?

George finds it difficult because of the Manager's presence

George To tell you something!
Richard What?
George About *me.*

As George says "me" he surreptitiously points to Richard who is confused. George moves in front of the Manager to Richard

I'm a *doctor.* That's *me. Doctor—me.*

He points surreptitiously to Richard and smiles back at the Manager who has been watching George flick his finger in the direction of Richard's crutch

Me. GP. That's *me. Me* NC—GP.

He points surreptitiously to Richard and smiles at the Manger who is becoming suspicious of the gesture

That's me. GP. Go see.

George hesitatingly moves in front of the Manager towards the lift then stops as Richard still looks blank

Yep. Best *doctor* in Norwich.

He flicks his finger in front of the Manager towards Richard. The Manager thinks George is going to attack his "parts" so clutches himself

Excuse me! (*He hurries to the lift and presses the button. He suddenly remembers something*) Oo!

Both Richard and the Manager clutch themselves as George hurries back

And I think *somebody* should remember to tell their *friends* about me. Yes. *Christmas* is *in* and *Easter* is going to be a little late this year. (*He collects his briefcase and hurries into the lift*) Ah! (*Calling to Richard*) And there's no hurry for you to get upstairs. I've got some sorting out to do. Yes. I'll give you a complete diagnosis when I see you. I think it could be terminal!

George departs

Richard and the Manager are transfixed. Music

The set changes to become the lounges of suites 648 and 650

The two elegant lounges are identical in shape but differ in furniture and colour. The lounge of 650 occupies L. *It has a door in the rear wall leading to the corridor and a door in the* L *wall leading to the bedroom.* R *of the door into the corridor and at right angles to it is the bathroom door through which can be seen part of the bathroom. There is a phone on a low table below the bathroom door with a chair by it and a pouffe below the bedroom door*

The lounge of 648 occupies R. *It has a door in the rear wall leading to the corridor and a door in the R wall leading to the bedroom. L of the door to the corridor and at right angles to it is the bathroom door through which can be seen part of the bathroom. There is a phone on a low table below the bathroom door with a chair by it and a pouffe below the bedroom door. Please see ground plan B on page 90*

During the revolve, the action in the reception area continues and at the same time as the two lounges appear, the action in that area commences as Pamela hurries into 648 lounge from the corridor. She closes the door and leans against it, dramatically

Pamela Can I go through with it? (*After a very brief pause*) Yes!

There is a knock on the corridor door. She looks at her watch

(*To herself*) Impatient! (*Opening the door; huskily*) Doctor Christmas, I presume.

Maria, the young Spanish chambermaid, enters with the household trolley, which she leaves in the doorway. Maria is gorgeous with a nervous giggle. Her uniform is mainly white

Maria (*giggling*) 'Scusa, madam.
Pamela Oh. Yes.
Maria I make up bed, si?
Pamela Er—yes. Fine.

Maria giggles and exits into the bedroom R

Pamela looks at her watch and then goes to the phone and dials

(*On the phone*) Hello, is that reception? ... It's Mrs Willey in six-four-eight. I was talking to one of your guests just now. Dr Christmas. I was wondering if you could tell me his room number. ... Thank you. (*Suddenly realizing*) Did you say six-fifty? That's next door to six-four-eight, isn't it? ... Oh, nothing. Very handy having a doctor next door. ... No, I'm fine but you never know what may develop. (*She replaces the receiver*)

Maria comes out of the bedroom. During the following, George enters timorously into the lounge of 650 from the corridor and stands there for a second, still holding his briefcase in one hand and the door key in the other

Maria Change towels, si?
Pamela Yes.
Maria In bathroom?
Pamela Thank you.

Maria takes the towels from the trolley and exits into the bathroom. Pamela exits into 648 bedroom

George puts his briefcase down and goes to the phone. He checks with the hotel information sheet for the number of room service and dials

As he does so, Maria comes out of 648 bathroom with dirty towels and puts them on the trolley

Maria (*calling in the direction of 648, bedroom*) Thank you, madam.
Pamela (*off*) Thank you!

Maria exits to the corridor, closing the door

George (*on the phone*) Hello, room service. It's Christmas in six-fifty. . . .
No, no. *Doctor* Christmas. I'd like to order some champagne and
sandwiches. . . . Vintage? No, I want fresh ones. . . . Oh, the champagne.
No. Just ordinary. And two rounds of smoked salmon sandwiches. Dr
Noel Christmas, suite six-fifty. . . . Thank you. (*He puts the phone down*)

Maria enters 650 lounge with her trolley, which she leaves in the doorway

Maria Scusa, señor!
George Ah! Yes?
Maria (*giggling*) You new guest, six-fifty, si?
George *Si*—yes.
Maria (*looking at her pad*) Dr and Mrs Christmas.
George Yes.
Maria (*looking at her pad, giggling*) Afternoon only.
George (*awkwardly*) Yes—two and a half hours.

> *During the next lines, Pamela enters 648 lounge from the bedroom. She is
> now wearing a very revealing nightdress. She looks at her watch, goes to the
> phone, dials 650 and then sits by the phone*

Maria Towels for bathroom?
George Thank you very much. You—er—you won't be popping in and out
all afternoon, will you?
Maria (*giggling*) No.
George Jolly good.

Maria exits into 650 bathroom

*George moves to go as the phone rings. He hesitates for a moment or two and
then apprehensively picks it up*

(*On the phone, tentatively*) Hello?
Pamela (*on the phone, in a low sexy voice*) Is that Dr Christmas?

George looks blank

George (*on the phone*) Er—who is this?
Pamela (*on the phone, seductively*) Mrs Christmas.
George (*on the phone, blankly*) Mrs——? (*Realizing that it must be Jennifer*)
Oh! Hey! Your telephone number's been engaged for ages.

Pamela looks in surprise at her phone

Pamela (*on the phone, bemused*) Has it?
George (*on the phone*) Are you phoning from somewhere in the hotel?
Pamela (*on the phone, surprised*) Yes.
George (*on the phone*) Well, listen. You find your way to room six-fifty——
Pamela (*on the phone, sexily*) Yes?

George (*on the phone*) And then the moment you get here——
Pamela (*on the phone, quickly*) You'll make mad passionate love to me!

George's face goes blank as he takes in this outrageous suggestion. He blinks and looks at the phone

George (*on the phone*) I shall do no such thing.
Pamela (*on the phone, laughing*) Teaser!
George (*on the phone*) As soon as you get here——
Pamela (*on the phone*) Yes?
George (*on the phone*) I shall leave.

Pamela's face goes blank as she takes this in. She then thinks George must have been joking

Pamela (*on the phone, laughing*) You're dreadful!
George (*on the phone*) Look where exactly are you? Reception?
Pamela (*on the phone*) No, I'm in room six-four-eight, of course.
George (*on the phone*) Good, all you . . . (*He realizes*) Six-four-eight? You're in six-four-eight?
Pamela (*on the phone*) Yes.
George (*on the phone*) You can't be!
Pamela (*on the phone*) I am!
George (*on the phone*) How did you get in there?!
Pamela (*on the phone*) Just walked in.
George (*on the phone*) But Mr Willey's *wife*!
Pamela (*on the phone*) I know I am. So what.
George (*on the phone*) So——? (*He suddenly realizes he's been talking to Pamela. On the phone, foolishly laughing*) Hello, Mrs Willey.
Pamela (*on the phone*) Are you all right, George?
George (*on the phone*) Oh, yes! I'm raring to go.

Maria comes out of bathroom with dirty towels

Maria Scusa.
George (*jumping*) Oo!
Pamela (*on the phone*) What is it?
George (*on the phone*) It's all right, it's the chamberlain—the chambermaid. Hang on. (*To Maria*) What is it?
Maria I do things in bedroom?
George Don't bother.
Maria I no turn bed down.
George No. They're not going to stay long. *We're* not.

Maria doesn't understand

Dr, Mrs Christmas, in-out.

Maria doesn't understand

Me. Speedy Gonzales!
Maria (*understanding*) Ah, si!

Maria exits into the corridor, leaving the door open

George (*on the phone*) Sorry about that, Mrs Willey.
Pamela (*on the phone*) I'm wearing that naughty nightie, George.
George (*on the phone*) You mustn't catch cold.

Pamela laughs

Pamela (*on the phone*) I'll come over, shall I?

Richard storms into 650 from the corridor, closing the door behind him

Richard I ask you!
George (*jumping*) Ah!

In 648 Pamela reacts to George's "Ah!"

Pamela (*on the phone*) What is it?
Richard Would you believe it?

George has put the receiver in his trouser pocket and nonchalantly folded his arms

George Sh, sh, sh!
Richard Never mind "sh, sh, sh"! Jennifer's number's not engaged, it's out of order.
George Sh, sh, sh!
Richard Out of bloody order!
George SSSSH!
Pamela (*on the phone*) George?!

Richard suddenly notices the bulge in George's pocket

Richard What's that?
George Mm. (*He looks down and reacts to finding the receiver in his pocket. He removes it*) Oh, yes. Just making a call.
Richard Who to?
George Room service. For you. (*On the phone*) Thank you, it all sounds very appetizing.
Pamela (*on the phone*) What does?
George (*on the phone*) The little tit-bits. But Dr Christmas is not in any hurry. And put a little slice of lemon on it, will you. (*He replaces the receiver*)

During the ensuing dialogue, Pamela frowns and exits into 648 bedroom

Richard No hurry? That's a damn silly thing to say to *this* room service.
George Please call it off. The portents are against you, Mr Willey.

Richard picks up the phone and dials. During the following speech George gets increasingly more worried

Richard It's not the portents, it's British Telecom. Poor Jennifer will be sitting there thinking I've gone off her. (*On the phone*) Reception? Can you get hold of one of those messenger fellows on a motor bike? . . . Excellent. Take this down . . . Bristow, 34a Sloane Square. Message reads:

"Your phone out of order. Sir Charles Easter needs you. Suite six-fifty *Westminster Hotel*. Come immediately."

George No, *Christmas*.

Richard I'm not waiting that long.

George grabs the phone

George (*on the phone*) Hang on a second. (*To Richard*) We're not Sir Charles Easter. We're Dr Noel Christmas.

Richard Oh yes! (*Grabbing the phone*) We're not Sir Charles Easter, we're Dr Noel Christmas. (*He puts the phone down*) Right, thanks, George. Where's the key to this suite?

Richard hands George his briefcase

George There.

George gives him the key

Richard Lovely. Just hang on a second till I get back, will you?

George (*surprised*) Where're you going?

Richard My suite next door.

George grabs Richard, horrified

George No!

Richard To change into my pyjamas.

George *No!* You mustn't be seen wandering around corridors. (*Suddenly*) You're supposed to be at the Home Office.

Richard (*hesitating*) Yes, that's true. *You* go and get them.

George Oh! I—er I wasn't planning to go next door, actually.

Richard God, you're nervous, George. Anyone would think *you* were having it off with somebody else's wife.

Richard laughs. George does his best to join in as he glances in the direction of 648. Richard sneezes

> *During the next two lines, Pamela comes out of 648 bedroom wearing the nightie and a matching négligé, goes out of suite 648 and into the corridor. The door closes behind her*

George Bless you!

Richard Blasted hay fever. My pills are in six-four-eight bathroom somewhere.

George I'll get them for you.

Richard Thank you.

> *Richard exits into 650 bedroom as:*

George opens the corridor door

> *Pamela steps in*

George Out! (*He pushes Pamela out into the corridor and slams the door*)

> *Pamela exits as the bedroom door to 650 opens and Richard comes in*

(*Swatting the air*) Out! Out! (*To Richard*) Damn mosquitoes.
Richard You're not as bright as you think you are, George.
George (*weakly*) What?
Richard How were you planning to get into six-four-eight?
George Knock on the door.
Richard There's nobody there to let you in.

George hesitates and then gives a silly laugh

Here's the key, you fathead.

Richard gives him the key and then sneezes. George glances nervously at the corridor door

George SSSSH!
Richard Getting worse. Don't forget my pills.
George (*quietly*) Pills, yes. (*He pushes Richard towards the bedroom*)
Richard And don't forget my pyjamas.
George (*quietly*) Pyjamas, yes. (*He pushes Richard into 650 bedroom and closes the door*)

Richard exits

There is an immediate knock on the corridor door. George freezes and then puts the briefcase between his legs and holds the handle of the bedroom door in his left hand and the handle of the corridor door in his right hand. He hesitates nervously between the two doors. Then he throws open the corridor door while still holding on to the handle of the bedroom door

(*Opening the corridor door*) I'm sorry, Mrs Will——! (*He stops*)

The Chinese Waiter comes in pushing the trolley on which are champagne and sandwiches

You're not Mrs Will!
Waiter No. Mr Wong. Champagne, sandwiches—Dr Christmas.
George (*whispering*) Where's the lady?
Waiter Lady?
George Lady outside in naughty nightie.
Waiter Oh! I come—she run.
George Good.
Waiter You Dr Christmas?
George Dr Christmas, yes.
Waiter Sign, please.

The telephone rings. George hesitates and looks nervously at the bedroom door

(*Indicating the phone*) Ding bell.
George Yes! (*He puts his briefcase down and answers the phone*)

During the ensuing phone conversation the Waiter, to George's annoyance, gets increasingly interested

(*On the phone, nervously*) Hello? . . . (*Quietly urgent*) Mrs Willey, stay in your room. . . . Locked yourself out. Where are you then? . . . No, I don't know where the chambermaid's cupboard is. Mrs Willey, you shouldn't be wandering around the corridors in your nightie. . . . No, don't come back here! I'll go next door to six-four-eight and then I'll be able to let you in. . . . I've got a key. . . . How? Well, your hu——(*He stops as he realizes, madly thinking*) Your hu—your hu—your hu—your hubsolutely right, I haven't got a key. I'm going to borrow a key from the waiter. (*He replaces the receiver, picks up his briefcase and moves to go*)

Waiter You want pass key for next room?
George (*moving*) No thank you.
Waiter You sign please, Dr Christmas.
George In a minute. I'll be back. Pyjamas, pills.
Waiter (*confused*) Pyjamas, pills.

George hurries out of suite 650 into the corridor. Richard comes out of 650 bedroom wearing his underpants, shirt and socks and carrying his trousers

The Waiter looks suitably surprised

Richard Ah! Well, don't stand there gaping! Take that in there.
Waiter (*blankly*) Trolley to bedroom?

As the Waiter pushes the trolley into 650 bedroom, George enters into 648 lounge from the corridor, letting himself in with the key. He leaves the door open. George looks around nervously wondering which door is the bedroom door. George exits to 648 bedroom as the Waiter returns from 650 bedroom

Richard (*to the Waiter*) You can toddle off.
Waiter No. Dr Christmas must sign.

Richard goes to sign

No! *Dr Christmas* must sign. He tell me wait.
Richard (*realizing*) Oh! Did he?
Waiter He gone next door, six-four-eight.
Richard Er—yes, I know that.
Waiter You gentleman from six-four-eight, yes?
Richard Er—no. No, not me.
Waiter You no Willey?
Richard No. Me no Willey.
Waiter After lunch. In lobby. You order three pot coffee with wife.
Richard No. I didn't order three pot coffee with wife. I don't have a wife.
Waiter No six-four-eight. No wife.
Richard No six-four-eight. No wife. I'm here in six-fifty. Sir Charles Easter.
Waiter Easter. (*He looks at the bill*) Six-fifty—Dr Noel Christmas.
Richard Yes. I'm sharing.
Waiter (*blankly*) Sharing?
Richard With Dr Christmas—Noel.
Waiter Oh.
Richard Noel, my friend.
Waiter (*thinking he realizes*) Ah, *friend*!

He smiles lasciviously at Richard and looks down at Richard's legs. Richard proceeds to put his trousers on

Richard Yes. Just good friends, understand.

Waiter Oh yes, me understand, good friend. You very like three pot coffee gentleman.

Richard No, I'm definitely Charlie Easter.

Waiter Charlie Easter.

Richard You remember that.

Waiter Charlie Easter.

Richard I don't remind you of anybody else.

Waiter Anybody else?

Richard Yes. For instance, famous British politician Richard Willey.

Waiter Who he?

Richard (*coldly*) Thank you. Look, I'll sign that. Noel won't mind. (*He takes the bill and signs*)

Waiter OK. You and Noel share and share alike, eh?

Richard Yes. (*He takes a £10 note from his pocket*) And—er—I'm sure you'll be able to keep mum.

Waiter (*pleased*) Oh, yes. This keep Mum and whole family.

The Waiter exits into the corridor

Richard goes to the phone and dials

George comes out of 648 bedroom with his briefcase, Richard's pyjamas, slippers and dressing-gown

The phone rings in 648 lounge. George hesitates momentarily then puts his briefcase down and answers the phone

George (*on the phone, whispering violently*) I'm coming!

Richard (*on the phone*) What are you doing for God's sake?

George (*on the phone*) I couldn't find your pyjamas.

Richard (*on the phone*) Well, hurry up! (*He sneezes*)

George (*on the phone*) Oh, pills!

Richard Same to you! (*He slams the phone down*)

Richard goes into 650 bedroom

George, leaving his briefcase, goes into 648 bathroom

Pamela enters 648 lounge from the corridor and exits into 648 bedroom

George enters from 648 bathroom with the pills and exits into the corridor, closing the door behind him

Pamela enters from 648 bedroom and exits into 648 bathroom

Richard, carrying a glass of champagne, enters 650 lounge from the bedroom and moves to the phone again

George enters 650 lounge from the corridor

Richards puts his champagne down

George Here we are.

Richard I thought you'd been out to buy a pair.

George I'm doing my level best, Mr Willey!

Richard I'm sorry, George, I'm sorry.

George Dressing-gown, slippers . . . And there's your key to next door.

Richard Did you get my pills?

George Yes I did. (*He hands the bottle to Richard*)

Richard Thank you, George. You've proved yourself a good friend.

George (*glancing in the direction of suite 648*) Yes, well, I'm closer to you than you think.

Richard Right then, you'd better get back on the job.

George (*startled*) What?

Richard You'd better get back to the Home Office.

George Oh yes! I'm on my way.

Richard Tell Doubleday to take the chair. (*He stops*) Where's your brief-case?

George What?

Richard Your briefcase with all the papers.

George (*realizing*) Oh! I must have left it next door.

Richard Here's the key. Go and get it.

Richard pushes George but George resists

George Do I have to?

Richard Of course you do. Leave the key at reception. (*He pushes George into the corridor and picks up his champagne*)

George exits

(*To himself*) Come on, Jennifer. I'm ready, willing and . . . (*He sneezes. This makes him shoot his champagne in the air which he attempts to catch in his glass*)

Richard exits into 650 bedroom

George enters 648 lounge from the corridor and moves to get his briefcase

Pamela enters from 648 bathroom carrying a glass scent-spray

Pamela George!

George Ah!! (*He sticks his hands into the air*)

Pamela (*laughing*) Do you think everyone having affairs has as much fun as this?

George Fun?

Pamela I'm having a ball.

George I think I'm having a heart attack.

Pamela Don't look so worried, George. What are you going to be like when we actually get into bed together?

George Absolutely useless.

Pamela No you won't.

George I will. I don't think I can function under these circumstances.

Pamela Nothing too disastrous has happened yet.

George But it will.

Pamela Relax! Now come on.

George Where?

Pamela Next door to your suite.

George No! Let me go first.

Pamela Why?

George See everything's all right. I want it to be perfect. Room temperature. Champagne temperature. My temperature. I want to slip into my "jarmy boos" and my dressing-gown and look all laid and cool back.

Pamela laughs

Pamela You're not used to this, are you?

George It shows does it?

Pamela Silly boy. Come on.

George No! You've got to stay here until I ring through. And if I don't ring through it's because I've dropped dead.

Pamela George!

George It could happen. I'm very excitable. And if I have a heart attack or a fit or something you mustn't get involved. Let the management sort it out.

Pamela You're not going to have a heart attack.

George I might.

Pamela Come on.

George No! I've just remembered.

Pamela What?

George Something cropped up.

Pamela Next door?

George Something rather nasty.

Pamela What?

George Mice.

Pamela Mice?

George Dozens of them.

Pamela At the *Westminster Hotel*?

George Yes, you'd think the price would put them off. You stay here. I'll go and report it to reception.

Pamela George, never mind the mice! You're not the Pied Piper of Hamelin.

George I know, but to have mice——

Pamela (*interrupting*) Forget the mice. Forget suite six-fifty. One of us has clearly got to take the initiative.

George Let's toss for it.

Pamela Relax. (*She removes his jacket, pulling it down from the shoulders so it is inside out, and puts it, and the scent spray on the table*)

George Oh, I am relaxed! I am. I am. (*Trying to fold his arms*) I am. I am relaxed.

During the ensuing dialogue she tantalizingly removes his waistcoat, his tie and unbuttons his shirt

Pamela Good. We've wasted enough time already. We've got this lovely suite here—all to ourselves. We don't need to go next door.

George (*protesting*) But you see, there's Mr Doubleday at the department——

Pamela Sssh. Forget about Mr Doubleday. You go into the bedroom, take all your clothes off and get into bed. And never mind about wearing pyjamas or anything else!

She untucks his shirt and pulls it down from his shoulders. George stands there for a moment, looking rather foolish

Oh, George!

George (*finally*) Well, I suppose Mr Doubleday can manage for a while.

Pamela Yes. Now, you get ready and I'll ring room service.

During the next speech she intersperses her words by squirting George's chest with the scent spray. It's cold and it tickles

I'll order—some iced—champagne ... (*Sexily*) The ice cubes can be fun, George.

As she finishes speaking she gives a final squirt of the spray down the top of his trousers. George leaps about partly in discomfort and partly in ecstasy

George Oooo! Mrs Willey ...!

Pamela Yes, George?

George You won't be long, will you?

George hurries into 648 bedroom

Pamela dials the number

Pamela (*on the phone*) This is six-four-eight. I'd like a bottle of vintage champagne, please. .... That sounds fine. And four dozen oysters and a little slice of lemon. (*She replaces the phone. Calling*) George!

George appears immediately. He is in underpants, shirt, socks and shoes and in the act of removing his trousers

George Yes?

Pamela Champagne and oysters are on the way.

George This is living.

Pamela Now, I'm going to have a quick bath—to freshen up.

George You're fresh enough already.

Pamela You won't go off the boil, will you?

George No, I think I'm simmering rather nicely.

George exits into 648 bedroom

Pamela picks up George's jacket, waistcoat, tie and briefcase and exits into 648 bathroom

Richard, sneezing violently, enters 650 lounge from 650 bedroom with the bottle of pills. He is wearing pyjamas, dressing-gown and slippers

Richard (*to himself*) Damn pills aren't working. (*He swallows a few more tablets*)

Richard exits into 650 bathroom

Pamela enters 648 lounge from 648 bathroom

Pamela George—will you scrub my back, please George?

Pamela exits into 648 bathroom

George enters from 648 bedroom. He is in his underpants, shoes and socks, carrying his trousers

George Oh my goodness! Don't worry I'll keep my eyes closed.

George exits into 648 bathroom and locks the door

Richard enters 650 lounge from 650 bathroom. He is carrying the bottle of pills and a glass of water. He sneezes

Richard (*perplexed*) Bloody funny. (*He swallows a couple more tablets*)

There is a knock on 650 door. Richard opens the door to the corridor

Jennifer comes in from the corridor. She is wearing a bright red wig and large "feminine" sunglasses. Underneath she is a bright, pretty blonde in her mid-twenties. She is dressed in a white suit and a cream blouse. She hurries past him into the lounge

What the . . .?
Jennifer It's me, Mr Willey.
Richard Jennifer!

Jennifer takes off her wig and sunglasses and puts them on the phone table

Jennifer I got your message and dropped everything.
Richard Lovely! I would never have recognized you.
Jennifer That's the idea.
Richard You clever girl.

Richard, in his enthusiasm, starts to take off her jacket and unbutton the sleeves of her blouse

Jennifer You never know who you might bump into around here.
Richard That's good thinking, actually. Lily Chatterton happens to be staying in the hotel.
Jennifer Chilly Lily?
Richard That's the one.
Jennifer She'd certainly remember me.
Richard Well, you can forget about Downing Street for the next couple of hours.
Jennifer (*grinning*) I'll do my best.
Richard Lovely! (*He goes to embrace her but sneezes*)
Jennifer You haven't got a cold, have you?
Richard Blasted hay fever. Damn pills don't seem to be doing the trick either.

Jennifer takes the bottle from him

Usually clears it immediately.

Jennifer (*reading the label*) "Benzedrine"?

Richard No. Antihistamine.

Jennifer Says "Benzedrine".

Richard snatches the bottle and reads

Richard That bloody fool Pigden. Anti-depressants! These were prescribed for me after the Conservatives lost that last by-election.

Jennifer They're only pep pills. One of those won't harm you.

Richard I've just taken about half a dozen!

Jennifer (*close to him*) Could be interesting! How do you feel?

Richard Lovely! (*He goes to kiss her but sneezes violently*) I'd better go to my suite next door and get the proper pills.

Jennifer We're not in the next room to you and your wife, are we?

Richard Yes, Pigden fixed that too.

Jennifer I think I've been far smarter sending my husband to ski in Italy.

Richard Well, you're a clever girl. Pigden's a nincompoop. Hell, he's got the key to six-four-eight.

Jennifer Where is he?

Richard Half way to the Home Office by now. The key's at reception. I know! (*Going to the phone and dialling*) Help yourself to some champagne. In the bedroom.

Jennifer Lovely! Champagne's the only thing I can't resist. Up to now!

Jennifer exits into 650 bedroom

Richard Oo! (*On the phone*) Hello? Is that my friendly Oriental waiter? . . . Good. Sir Charles Easter here. . . . Yes, Dr Christmas good friend six-fifty. . . . I want you to let me into suite six-four-eight. . . . I know you shouldn't but I gave you a good tip, remember. For Mum . . . no, I don't want to disturb them at reception. You have pass key. . . . Good. . . . More money for Mum, yes, OK. You come now suite six-fifty. (*He puts the phone down*)

Jennifer enters from 650 bedroom. She has a large towel wrapped around her and is carrying a glass of champagne and a sandwich

Jennifer Here we are!

Richard Oo, you look absolutely——(*He sneezes*)

Jennifer Poor Mr Willey.

Richard It's Dr Christmas, actually.

Jennifer Yes, so your note said. I thought Mr Pigden was booking us in as Sir Charles and Lady Easter.

Richard For reasons best known to Pigden, he decided to change it to Dr and Mrs Christmas.

Jennifer goes close to him and gives him a sip of her drink

Jennifer Well, never mind whether it's Easter or Christmas, Mr Willey's going to get his little present.

Richard Yes, please!
Jennifer After I've had my bath.
Richard You don't need a bath.
Jennifer To freshen up.
Richard You're fresh enough as it is. Pristine! Pristine clean. (*He chuckles*) Pristine clean. (*He laughs again and stops*) Hey, I'd better not have any more champers! What with that and the Benzedrine, I'll be flying round the bedroom.
Jennifer As long as you know where to land. (*Sexily*) Where's the bathroom, Mr Willey?
Richard Through there.
Jennifer I won't be long.
Richard And I think it would be in order for you to call me Dickie.
Jennifer All right. You hurry up and get your pills—while I run my bath—Dickie. And I might ask you to scrub my back, Dickie.
Richard Oo!
Jennifer Lots and lots of soap.
Richard Oh, rather. Lots and lots of lather.

Jennifer goes into 650 bathroom

(*To himself, in ecstasy*) A fellow could slip off and break his neck.

There is a knock on the corridor door. Richard opens it

The Waiter steps in

Waiter Ah, Sir Charlie!
Richard Yes. You have key for six-four-eight.
Waiter Yes, please. Pass key. (*He holds out key with one hand and presents the other for his tip*)
Richard (*giving money*) OK.
Waiter Where your good friend, Dr Christmas?
Richard What? Oh, he's popped out. You let me in next door, come on.
Waiter You friend of guest next door, too. Yes?
Richard Yes. Good friend.

The bathroom door to 650 opens and Jennifer's head appears

Jennifer I'm ready to have my back——(*She stops on seeing the Waiter. Gaily*) Sorry! (*She closes the door*)

The Waiter looks at Richard

Richard That's Mrs Christmas.
Waiter (*amazed*) Mrs Christmas?
Richard Yes.
Waiter Doctor has wife?
Richard Yes!
Waiter She beautiful!
Richard Yes!
Waiter Doctor versatile.
Richard Never mind that!

Richard pushes the Waiter into the corridor and follows him out. He hurries into the corridor as the door to suite 648 is opened by the Waiter with his pass key. The Waiter enters 648 lounge followed by Richard

(*To the Waiter*) Thank you. You can go.

Waiter Sir Charlie—six-four-eight your friends, yes?

Richard Yes. Mr and Mrs Willey. Very good friends.

Waiter (*doubtfully*) You good friend of Mr or Mrs?

Richard None of your damn business! (*He pushes the Waiter out into the corridor and shuts the door*)

The Waiter exits

Richard goes to open 648 bathroom door. It is locked. Richard is puzzled and pushes the door. He rattles the handle

The door opens and George, wrapped in a towel, pops his head out. His arms have lather up to the elbow

George (*not realizing*) Just take the cork out, please.

George goes back into 648 bathroom, closing the door

Richard stands there dumbfounded

After a moment the door opens again and George's face, aghast, appears. George comes out and bangs the door closed

Richard Pigden!

George opens and closes his mouth, but no sound comes out

Why aren't you at the . . .? What are you doing in my . . .? Why are you dressed in . . .? Why don't you say something, Pigden?

George One question at a time, please.

Richard Pigden! Explain yourself.

George I'm here—in your suite—in your bathroom—in your towel . . .

Richard I can see all that!

George Yes. (*Forcefully*) I told you to stay next door.

Richard Never mind that! What are you doing in my bathroom with no clothes on?

George can only chuckle. Then he stops

George I beg your pardon?

Richard Why aren't you at the Home Office?

George I came back.

Richard What for?

George To go to the bathroom.

The bathroom door is pulled by the unseen Pamela. George pulls it shut

Richard (*amazed*) There's somebody else in there.

George Yes. That's why I came back. I had an appointment.

Richard What the hell are you talking about.

George An appointment—with a person.
Richard (*staggered*) In my bathroom?
George Yes.

Richard tries to take this in. After a moment Richard smiles lasciviously

Richard You've got a woman in there.
George No, I haven't!
Richard Yes, you have! You've got a woman in there!
George No, honestly, there's no woman in there, definitely. It's—it's a chap!
Richard (*nonplussed*) A chap?
George Yes. You know—a chap. A fellow. A chap.
Richard What the hell are you doing with a chap in my bathroom?
George (*after a moment of frantic thought*) You know!
Richard (*blankly*) What?
George You know.

He gives Richard a quick limp-wristed wave. The situation dawns on Richard, who is astonished

Richard You mean . . .? (*He repeats the gesture*)
George Yes.
Richard You and . . .? (*He indicates the bathroom and repeats the gestures once again*)
George Yes.
Richard Well, I—er—I don't know what to say, George. But it's a bit much, isn't it? You making assignations in my hotel room.
George I told you to stay next door.
Richard Yes, I can see why!

The door is pulled by Pamela. George pulls it shut

He's getting impatient.
George Yes. I was in the middle of scrubbing his back.

The door is pulled open. George pulls it shut. The door is pulled open again

(*Yelling through the door*) I'm talking to *Mr Willey*.

There is a fractional pause and then the door is hastily banged shut by the unseen Pamela. George quickly walks Richard away from the bathroom door

Richard (*finally*) My name certainly did the trick there.
George Yes. He knows he shouldn't be up here.
Richard Well, who the devil is he?
George What?
Richard Your chap! Who is he?
George Just a chap.
Richard (*blankly*) A chap.
George Yes. Ted.
Richard Ted?

George Yes. Ted.
Richard How did you come to meet a chap called Ted?
George At the office.
Richard Office? (*Surprised*) You mean the Home Office?
George Er—no. The Foreign Office.
Richard (*more surprised*) Ted's in the FO?
George Yes, the FO.
Richard Do I know Ted?
George Oh, no. He's very low grade.
Richard What's his position then?

George looks blank for a moment

George He's the tea boy.

Richard takes this in

Richard You're having a homosexual relationship with a tea boy in the FO?
George Yes.
Richard And he's in my bathroom?
George Yes.
Richard Making the tea, I suppose.
George No.
Richard God Almighty, George, none of this came out when you were positively vetted.
George I've kept it dark.
Richard But you've never shown any signs or anything.
George Well, I've decided to come out of the closet.
Richard What about Ted?
George No, he's staying inside the closet.
Richard (*moving away, angrily*) The whole question of government security comes into it. You're being more blatant about it than Burgess and MacLean!
George (*retaliating*) You're a fine one to talk! What about you and Mrs Bristow?!
Richard That is a very beautiful relationship.
George Well, so's mine with Ted!
Richard (*coolly*) I'll discuss this with you in the morning, Pigden. In the meantime I'd like *you* to return to the Home Office and look after that delegation and I'd like *Ted* to get back to the FO and look after his tea trolley.
George Yes.
Richard And before you go perhaps you'd kindly ask Ted if I could have my hay fever tablets.
George I gave them to you.
Richard You gave me Benzedrine.
George Oh dear. Thank goodness you didn't take any.
Richard I've swallowed half a dozen!
George Bloody hell! How do you feel?
Richard Murderous! Just get my hay fever tablets!

George opens the bathroom door as little as possible

George (*calling*) Excuse me, Ted . . .

George squeezes in and closes the door behind him

The Waiter enters 648 from the corridor pushing the trolley on which are champagne and oysters

Waiter Six-four-eight.
Richard What have you got there?
Waiter Champagne and four dozen oyster.
Richard I didn't order that.
Waiter No. You six-fifty.
Richard (*confused*) What? Oh, yes.
Waiter This for six-four-eight.
Richard 1969 vintage. Can't be.
Waiter Oh, yes.

George still in his towel comes out of the bathroom with the pills, closing the door

George Ted's in a state of shock. I've got the right pills this time.

Richard snatches the pills

Richard (*to George*) Did you order champagne and oysters?
Waiter No. He Dr Christmas from six-fifty.
Richard (*angrily*) I know that!
Waiter Champagne, oyster for six-four-eight.
George (*realizing*) Oh, yes. Ted must have ordered it.
Richard Ted?
Waiter Excuse please.
Richard (*impatiently*) What is it?
Waiter Who Ted?

Richard looks up to heaven

Richard (*tersely*) What?
Waiter Who Ted order champagne and oyster?
Richard Ted his friend.

The Waiter advances admonishingly on George

Waiter Ted, your friend?
George Yes.
Waiter (*pointing to Richard*) He your friend.
George Me very friendly.
Waiter Me no understand.
Richard Join the club.
Waiter You two gentlemen next door in six-fifty.
Richard Yes!
Waiter (*to George*) You Noel?
George Yes.

Waiter (*to Richard*) And you Charlie?

Richard That sums me up.

Waiter If you Noel and Charlie from six-fifty, why you in six-four-eight with no clothes on?

Richard Mind your own bloody business!

Waiter You no talk me like that!

The Waiter leaps into a threatening kung-fu pose. Richard hides beside George

Richard (*finally*) You clear off.

Waiter Who sign bill?

Richard (*looking at George*) Charge it to the Foreign Office.

The Waiter exits angrily into corridor muttering in Chinese

I'm going back to look after Jennifer.

George Jennifer? Oh, she got here, good.

Richard No thanks to you. You grab Ted and clear off, you sex maniac.

Richard exits into the corridor, closing the door

George looks doleful

648 bathroom door opens and Pamela appears

Pamela That was close!

George It was awful!

Pamela (*laughing*) Fancy Richard forgetting his pills.

George He thinks I'm having an affair with a tea boy from the Foreign Office.

Pamela A perfect cover-up. Has Richard gone back to work?

George (*sharply*) What?

Pamela Has Richard gone back to the Home Office?

George Oh! Er—yes. But he might return again.

Pamela No, he'll have his hands full for the rest of the day.

George looks in the direction of 650

George Yes, that's true.

Pamela So—er—where were we?

George Mrs Willey—I think I've gone off the boil now.

Pamela Oh, no.

George I'm sorry.

Pamela Well, come on let's see if we can get the fire going a bit.

Pamela takes an unhappy-looking George into 648 bedroom

Richard enters suite 650 from the corridor, closing the door behind him. He knocks on the bathroom door. Jennifer, dressed in a towel, opens the door

Jennifer Get your pills?

Richard Yes. Got a bit of a shock, too. George Pigden in my bathroom.

Jennifer Well, that's all right, isn't it?

Richard Scrubbing a tea boy from the Foreign Office.

Jennifer What?

Jennifer and Richard exit into 650 bathroom as George, still in his towel, comes out of 648 bedroom into the lounge

George (*speaking to the unseen Pamela*) I really think I ought to put the "Do Not Disturb" sign on the door.

Pamela appears in 648 bedroom doorway in her nightie

Pamela Is that absolutely necessary?
George Definitely.
Pamela Well, hurry up.
George If it's worth having, it's worth waiting for. (*He pushes her into 648 bedroom*)

Pamela exits

George shuts the bedroom door, then opens the corridor door and bends down to hang the sign on the outside door knob

The Manager is standing in the doorway about to knock

He stands there for a second as George freezes with the sign hovering around the Manager's crutch. George then holds the sign up against himself and indicates that the Manager should depart. The Manager storms past George

Manager Is either Mr or Mrs Willey in, please?

George looks nervously at the bedroom door

George Er—no.
Manager Then may I ask what you're doing in their room, Dr Christmas?
George I'm afraid not. The Hippocratic Oath and all that.

George indicates for the Manager to leave but the Manager glares at him

Manager Dr Christmas . . . !
George Ssh!
Manager Dr Christmas. One of my waiters has just come to me with a complaint.
George I'll see him at my surgery in the morning.

George goes to escort the Manager to the door but once again, the Manager does not budge

Manager I couldn't quite gather what he was going on about but it appears to have something to do with *two male friends* of yours, Ted and Charlie.
George Yes, Ted and Charlie. My two male friends.
Manager Well, normally I don't interfere with the guests——
George Quite right, nasty habit.

George indicates for the Manager to go. Yet again, the Manager glares at George

Manager —but I feel I should remind you that you booked in with your wife.

George Yes, well, she's next door.
Manager Then I'd be grateful if you'd return to her.
George We've had a bit of a ding dong.
Manager *Now.*
George But we've had a bit of a ding——
Manager *Now!*
George *Now!* (*He goes to exit but immediately returns*) I think I've locked myself out.
Manager (*firmly*) I have a key.

The Manager takes out his bunch of keys and exits purposefully past George into the corridor

George Oh, my God! (*He goes to knock on the bedroom door but decides that it's more urgent to get to suite 650*)

George hurries into the corridor

Richard comes out of 650 bathroom. He is now wearing slippers and just his pyjama trousers. He is carrying a towel and he is covered in soap bubbles. He is giggling and waving at the unseen Jennifer

The Manager enters into 650 lounge behind Richard and leaves the door open

The Manager is astonished. After a moment Richard sees the Manager and hastily closes the bathroom door

Manager Mr Willey! What on earth are you doing in here!

George hurries into 650 lounge from the corridor

George (*entering; to the Manager*) Well, thanks for letting me in——(*He sees Richard*) Oh, no! (*He stops as he takes in the situation. Then he goes to the pouffe* DL *and sits*)

There is a pause as the Manager looks from Richard to George

Richard (*finally, dramatically*) Oh, my God, he's come back.
George (*bemused*) Come back?
Richard (*to the Manager*) Thank God you got here. (*Pointing to George*) That lunatic tried to kidnap me!

The Manager looks at George. George looks about wondering who Richard is referring to, then he reacts as he realizes Richard means him

Manager (*bemused*) Dr Christmas?
Richard More like Dr Crippen. He invited me into his room and then shut me in his bathroom.
Manager (*advancing on George*) Is this true?

George opens his mouth to speak but Richard quickly steps in

Richard Of course it is! He sounded so plausible, too. He said he wanted to talk to me about how things worked, (*pointedly*) at the *Foreign Office.*

Especially the *tea breaks*. (*He does a hasty limp-wristed wave for George's benefit*)

Manager (*to George*) Did you shut Mr Willey in your bathroom?

George hesitates

George (*weakly*) I think I probably did, yes.

The bathroom door to 650 opens and Jennifer appears dressed in a towel

Jennifer Are you going to dry my——

Richard throws his towel over her as the Manager turns

Richard (*to Jennifer*) Get back in there! Go on! Back!

Richard pretends that Jennifer is trying to pull him into the bathroom. He has a brief but dramatic "struggle" with her in the doorway of the bathroom while the Manager and George look on, transfixed. Finally, exhausted, he pushes her back into the bathroom

Hand me my dressing-gown!

She does

And I suggest you take a cold shower, madam. (*He puts on the dressing-gown*)

Jennifer exits

Manager Who on earth . . .?
Richard That's the doctor's wife.
Manager Mrs Christmas?
Richard Lucky you were here or she'd have seduced me.
Manager No!
Richard Yes. She's as perverted as he is. After he'd shut me in the bathroom, his wife came in, took off all her clothes and made me scrub her back!
Manager Good God! (*He picks up the wig; surprised*) What on earth . . .?
Richard (*taking the wig*) That's what he was wearing when he grabbed me.

Richard sticks the wig on the outraged George's head. The bemused Manager picks up the sunglasses

Those, too.

Richard puts them on George. The Manager surveys George sternly

Manager (*to George*) Doctor, you will remain here. I'll see you back to your room, Mr Willey.
George (*rising; aghast*) No! That's not necessary.
Manager Sit!

George sits

After you, Mr Willey.
George (*rising*) No! (*Wildly*) I haven't tidied up in there.

Manager It's not your job to tidy up Mr Willey's room!
George Yes it is!

Richard takes the wig and sunglasses from George

Richard I think it's wiser if I return to my room, Doctor. (*Pointedly
referring to Ted*) And if I find anything I shouldn't I'll soon sweep it out!
George No!
Manager Sit!

George sits

And *stay*!

Richard and the Manager exit to the corridor

George opens the bathroom door of 650

George Quickly, Mrs Bristow.

Jennifer comes out in a towel

Jennifer Good-afternoon, Mr Pigden. Snap! (*She tugs at his towel*)
George Never mind that. Where are your clothes?
Jennifer (*surprised*) In the bedroom.
George Come on. (*He leads her towards 650 bedroom*)
Jennifer What's the matter?
George There'll be all hell let loose here in a minute.
Jennifer Why?
George I don't think Mr Willey's going to be too pleased when he discovers
that my tea boy is Mrs Willey.
Jennifer Mrs Willey—I thought she was out.
George She came back.
Jennifer What for?!
George Never you mind, but whatever it is, she hasn't had it.

George pushes Jennifer into 650 bedroom, follows her in and closes the door

The set changes to become the bedroom and lounge of suite 648

*The lounge moves to L and the bedroom occupies R. The bedroom has a window
L, with a dressing-table set into it, and a double bed below this. There is a fitted
wardrobe in the back wall. Please see ground plan C on page 91. In the lounge,
the doors to the corridor, bathroom and bedroom are all closed*

In 648 bedroom, Pamela is sitting up in bed in a nightie reading a magazine

*As the set starts to change, the door from the corridor into 648 lounge opens
and the Manager comes in followed by Richard*

Richard Thank you so much. Bye, bye.
Manager The doctor's due to leave shortly. And I do apologize for this
most unfortunate situation.
Richard (*grandly*) Say no more. It's all part of life's rich pageant.
Manager You've taken it remarkably well, Mr Willey.

Richard (*chuckling*) Yes, I don't know if it's the champagne or the overdose of Benzedrine.

Manager (*surprised*) Benzedrine?

Richard Probably these wicked little hay fever tablets. (*He laughs merrily and pushes the bewildered Manager into the corridor*)

The Manager exits, leaving the door open

Richard puts the wig and sunglasses in the pockets of his dressing-gown and knocks on the bathroom door

(*Angrily calling*) Ted! Ted!

In the bedroom, Pamela puts on her négligé and decides to look for George

Richard opens the bathroom door and goes in, closing the door

Pamela opens the bedroom door and comes out into the lounge. She closes the door behind her

Pamela (*calling*) George! George!

Pamela sees the corridor door open and hurries out into the corridor, leaving the door open

Richard comes out of the bathroom into the lounge closing the door behind him

Richard Ted! (*He taps on the bedroom door*) Ted! (*He opens the bedroom door and goes in*)

Pamela returns to the lounge from the corridor, closing the door behind her

Richard is looking in the bedroom wardrobe for Ted

Pamela George! (*She opens the bathroom door*) George! (*She sees nobody in the bathroom so goes towards the bedroom*)

Richard closes the wardrobe door and goes to the foot of the bed, searching for Ted. Pamela comes into the bedroom, closing the door behind her. She and Richard see each other and remain frozen for several seconds, their minds racing but their faces blank

Richard ⎫
Pamela ⎭ (*finally together*) Darling!

They both feign delighted surprise, rush to each other and embrace

CURTAIN

ACT II

The same. The action is continuous

Richard and Pamela have their arms round each other. They are both madly trying to think how to play the situation

Richard Darling!
Pamela Darling! What a marvellous surprise!
Richard Yes, it's more than that!
Pamela I had no idea you were here.
Richard No, I had no idea either. That *you* were here.
Pamela Well!!
Richard Yes, well! I—you're *here*.
Pamela Yes. And *you're* here, darling.
Richard Yes. We're *here*!
Pamela Yes, *both* of us.
Richard Yes. And me too!
Pamela Yes. And I'm wearing—er ...
Richard So am I! Well—we're here!
Pamela Yes!

They sit on end of the bed

I thought you were at the Home Office.
Richard Yes, I was. I came back. My hay fever. Made me feel a fit bunny. (*Quickly*) I mean a bit funny.
Pamela Didn't the pills work?
Richard Pills?
Pamela You came back for them.
Richard (*worried*) Did I?
Pamela (*realizing her mistake*) I—I—I *think* you did, yes.
Richard What makes you say that?
Pamela I—er—I just—er—noticed that the bottle had gone from the bathroom, so assumed you must ...
Richard Oh, yes, I'd forgotten. I didn't stay long. Did you notice any—er—any—er—any*thing* else in the bathroom?

Pamela hesitates

Pamela No. Why?
Richard I just wondered if you'd been to the bathroom recently.
Pamela Not *very* recently, no.
Richard Fine, fine. Well, there's no need is there?
Pamela No. Anyway, your hay fever's gone.

Richard (*expansively*) Yes, half a dozen Benzedrine did the trick.
Pamela Benzedrine?

Richard hesitates

Richard Antihistamine.
Pamela Good. Half a dozen Benzedrine would probably blow your mind.

Richard laughs gaily but the laugh sounds slightly hysterical. He suddenly stops. From time to time the combined effect of the pills and the alcohol will manifest itself in this way

Richard (*casually*) How long have *you* been back, darling?
Pamela Oh, no more than a minute. I was sitting watching *Evita* and twang!
Richard *Evita* and *Twang*?
Pamela That wretched disc of mine went again.
Richard Oh, twang! (*Sympathetically*) Oh dear.
Pamela Yes. So I rushed back here—staggered back here—got undressed—as best as I could—and was just going to bed. And I—er—I didn't expect to find you here in your dressing-gown.
Richard No, I'm a bit surprised myself. Like I said, my hay fever got worse—even after the pills—so everybody at the department—especially the Home Secretary—insisted that I come back here—again—take some more pills and rest a bit.
Pamela Good idea.
Richard ⎫ (*together*) I don't quite see ...
Pamela ⎭

They both stop and indicate for the other to continue

(*Together*) I don't quite see ...

They both stop again and indicate for the other to continue

(*Together*) I don't quite see how we missed each other.

As he finishes speaking Richard unknowingly brings out the red wig from his pocket as he makes a gesture with his hand. Pamela looks at the wig

Pamela What's that, darling?
Richard What?

Pamela indicates the wig. He looks at it but doesn't noticeably react

What an extraordinary thing. Oh, yes! (*He laughs as he madly tries to think of an explanation*) It was being used at the rehearsal.
Pamela What rehearsal?

Richard hesitates but only fractionally

Richard The department is laying on a sort of show—sort of cabaret—just an internal thing for—er—for the fun of it. Doubleday was using this for his impersonation of Neil Kinnock. I must have accidentally walked off with it. (*He takes his other hand out of his pocket. He is holding Jennifer's sunglasses*)

Pamela looks at them—so does Richard

(*Casually*) I won't tell you about the sunglasses.
Pamela (*simply*) Why not?
Richard Well ...
Pamela The Home Secretary doing Edna Everage, is he?
Richard (*after a slight pause*) No. I bought these because of my hay fever. The bright light was making me sneeze—these were all I could get. (*He puts them on*) They look a bit feminine, don't they?
Pamela Yes, they do.
Richard Yes. (*He takes them off and puts them in the upturned wig*)
Pamela (*brightly changing the subject*) Let's have a glass of that champagne! (*She hurries towards the lounge*)
Richard What champagne?

Pamela stops

Pamela (*realizing*) I—I—I thought I saw a bottle in the lounge as I rushed through—(*quickly*)—staggered through.
Richard (*realizing*) Ah yes! Good lord! (*Casually*) Did *you* order it?
Pamela No! Did you?
Richard No! Probably compliments of the management.
Pamela Yes! Lovely! I'll get it.

Pamela goes into 648 lounge followed by Richard

During the following dialogue the set changes to become the lounges of suites 648 and 650

Richard No! You go back to bed. Make yourself comfy. Get yourself—er—ready for me.
Pamela Richard!
Richard Well, now we're both here we may as well.
Pamela Middle of the afternoon?
Richard (*gaily*) Why not? On the carpet if you like.
Pamela (*gaily*) Why not?
Richard Great!
Pamela Yes, great!
Richard Yes! It might even put your disc back.

Richard pushes Pamela back into 648 bedroom as the bedroom disappears

  Pamela exits

648 lounge is R *and 650 lounge is* L. *In 648 lounge Richard hesitates for a moment, and then hurries to the phone and dials*

  Jennifer enters 650 lounge from 650 bedroom, putting on her blouse. She starts to look for her wig. George follows her into 650 lounge from 650 bedroom. He is wearing his towel, shoes and socks as before.

George Will you please *go*, Mrs Bristow.
Jennifer When I've found my wig and glasses. I'm not going without my disguise.

George We'll all need a disguise when Mr Willey finds out that his wife is my boyfriend.

The phone in 650 lounge rings. George lifts the receiver

(*On the phone*) Yes?

Richard (*on the phone*) It's me!

George (*to Jennifer*) Oh, my God, it's him! (*On the phone*) I can assure you, Mr Willey, it's the first time for either me or for your——

Richard (*on the phone*) Shut up! I just found Mrs Willey sitting up in bed in her nightie.

George (*on the phone*) Please don't harm her.

Richard (*on the phone*) What the hell are you talking about? She's far more likely to harm me.

George looks puzzled for a moment

George (*to Jennifer*) It's either the pills or he's as big a fool as the backbenchers say he is.

Jennifer takes the phone

Jennifer (*on the phone*) It's all right, Dickie. We'll make it some other time.

Richard (*on the phone*) You dear sweet understanding girl.

Jennifer (*on the phone*) When I've found my wig and glasses I'll beat a hasty retreat.

Richard (*on the phone*) Marvellous! (*Realizing*) Oh, no!

Jennifer (*on the phone*) What is it?

George (*worried*) What is it?

Richard takes the wig from his pocket

Richard (*on the phone*) I've got your wig and glasses here.

Jennifer (*on the phone*) Well, it's too dangerous to go without wearing those.

George (*worried*) Without wearing what?

Jennifer (*on the phone*) Especially if Lily Chatterton is knocking about the hotel.

George's face falls

George (*horrified*) Mrs Chatterton?!

Jennifer (*to George*) Ssh!

Richard (*on the phone*) You'd better send Pigden in immediately.

Jennifer (*to George*) Mr Willey wants you to pop next door for my wig and glasses.

George grabs the phone

George (*on the phone*) You didn't tell me Mrs Chatterton was staying in the hotel.

Richard (*on the phone*) Of course I didn't! If I'd told you Mrs Chatterton was on the same floor as——

George (*on the phone, yelling*) Same floor!

Richard (*on the phone*) That's all right. Mrs Chatterton doesn't know you, does she?

George (*on the phone*) No, but I know all about Mrs Chatterton. What about her *Vice Bill*?!

Richard (*on the phone*) Pay it, George, pay it!

George ignores this

George (*on the phone*) If she gets a sniff of what you're up to she'll go straight to the Home Secretary. I *told* you this would happen.

Richard (*on the phone*) I'm more worried about my wife at the moment. Just get in here quickly. I'll leave the door open and the wig and glasses by the telephone.

George (*on the phone*) But I've only got a towel on. My clothes are all in your bathroom.

Richard (*on the phone*) That'll serve you right for seducing Ted in there. Just hurry up!

Richard slams the phone down and, during the ensuing dialogue opens 648 door into the corridor

George (*replacing the receiver*) Oh, dear.

Jennifer You're the best PPS in the world!

Jennifer goes into 650 bedroom

George gently opens 650 corridor door and peers out. He gently tiptoes into the corridor, leaving the door ajar

In 648 lounge, Richard has put the sunglasses by the phone and is just about to leave the wig

Pamela enters from 648 bedroom

Pamela Richard?

Richard Ah!

Richard quickly puts the wig behind him, between his buttocks. He turns to face Pamela showing a smiling innocent face—only the audience sees the wig wedged between his legs

Pamela I—er—I was wondering if anything had gone wrong?

Richard No! Everything's fine! Come on, darling! Champagne! Beddy-byes!

Richard takes the champagne bucket and glasses from the trolley and propels Pamela to the bedroom. Richard's movements are somewhat peculiar as he attempts to move without letting the wig fall from between his buttocks and at the same time, avoid turning his back on Pamela

Oh! I am looking forward to this!

Pamela So am I!

Pamela and Richard exit into 648 bedroom, closing the door behind them

George enters 648 lounge from the corridor and leaves the door open

He goes to the phone table for the wig and sunglasses and is perturbed to find only the sunglasses which he picks up and puts down again. He has a quick look around for the wig but decides to get his clothes from 648 bathroom

George exits into 648 bathroom, closing the door behind him

Richard enters from 648 bedroom with the wig still wedged between his buttocks. He backs into the lounge

Richard I won't be a moment, darling. (*Calling into the corridor*) George!

Pamela enters 648 lounge from the bedroom

She stands there for a moment looking at Richard's back view and the red wig between his legs. She taps his shoulder

(*Jumping and turning*) Ah! I was just putting the "Do Not Disturb" sign on the door. You get into bed, darling.

Pamela Come on, then.

Richard No, I'm just going for a quick stroll to get my strength up. (*He pushes Pamela into 648 bedroom*)

Pamela exits

(*Stepping into the corridor, calling*) George!

George enters from 648 bathroom (still in his towel), carrying his clothes, and, without seeing Richard or thinking, closes the corridor door

George stands there nervously for a moment then decides to listen at the bedroom door. As he approaches the bedroom door the handle of the corridor door is rattled from outside by Richard. George freezes. Richard knocks on the door. George doesn't know what to do. There is a louder knock on the door. George goes to the corridor door and bends down to look through the keyhole

Richard exits

Pamela enters behind George from 648 bedroom

Pamela (*seeing George*) George!

George (*leaping into the air*) Ah! (*His clothes go flying in all directions. He hastily starts to get dressed but because of his nervousness can't get his legs into his trousers*)

Pamela Where on earth have you been for the last half hour?

George (*after a brief pause*) I don't know.

Pamela You only popped out to put the "Do Not Disturb" notice on the door.

George I got lost.

Pamela Well, we'll have to postpone it, my sweet. Richard's come back.

George Yes, I ... (*Realizing he shouldn't know*) No!

Pamela Yes!

George (*off-hand*) Where—er—where is he?

Pamela I don't know. He keeps popping in and out of the bedroom.

George Are you trying to win the Daily Double?

Richard enters 650 lounge from the corridor. He leaves the door ajar

Richard George?

Richard exits into 650 bedroom, closing the door behind him

Pamela I don't know what's come over Richard.
George Why?
Pamela He's just taken a stroll down the corridor with a red wig.
George (*relieved*) Has he? That's all right then—I mean, how peculiar! Well, if he's taken a stroll with a red wig, I think I'll take a stroll with sunglasses. (*He nonchalantly takes the sunglasses and puts them on*)
Pamela Sunglasses?
George I don't want to be recognized.
Pamela As a matter of fact, they're Richard's.
George Are they really? He won't mind.
Pamela I'm so sorry about this afternoon, George. You'd better nip back next door quickly. (*She opens the corridor door*)

Lily is standing there about to knock

Lily (*surprised*) Oh. (*Entering*) I wondered if you might like to join me for a cup of . . .

Lily stops on seeing George who is standing there transfixed, in the act of doing up his trousers with his braces caught between his legs. His shirt isn't properly tucked in

Oh!

Lily looks from George to Pamela. Pamela pulls her négligé together

Pamela (*smoothly*) Do you two know each other?
Lily No.
Pamela (*indicating Lily*) This is Mrs Lily Chatterton, Member of Parliament.

George tries to smile and hurriedly puts his waistcoat on. He takes the sunglasses off and puts them in his pocket. He then realizes his flies are undone so quickly zips them up. He then extends his hand and shakes Lily's hand warmly

Lily How do you do.

George tries to say "how do you do" but no words come out. He coughs to clear his throat and then speaks hoarsely

George (*to Lily*) How do you do, Lady Chatterley—(*quickly*)—Mrs Chatterton!
Pamela (*indicating George*) And this is Dr Noel Christmas.

George turns away in anguish and then almost immediately turns back with a very polite smile on his face

Dr Christmas is our family doctor, aren't you?

George, who has been attempting to tie his tie, can only nod. He gives up trying to tie it and flings it nonchalantly around his neck

Whenever I'm in London the doctor likes to give me a check-up. Thank you so much for calling, Doctor.
Lily Where exactly is your practice, Doctor?
Pamela ⎱ *(together)* ⎰Harley Street.
George ⎰   ⎱Norwich.

Pamela and George exchange a quick glance. Then:

Pamela ⎱ *(together)* ⎰Norwich.
George ⎰   ⎱Harley Street.

Pamela and George exchange another glance

George *(to Lily)* Harley Street in Norwich. Do you know it?
Lily Can't say I do.

George, in a final attempt to look as though everything is normal, puts his jacket on. Unknown to him it's inside out. (NB.—from when Pamela removed it in Act I.) He stands there for a moment trying to nonchalantly slip his hands into the side pockets of his jacket—which unfortunately aren't there. Lily is mesmerized

(Finally) I might see you in the lounge for tea, Mrs Willey.
Pamela *(taking Lily to the door)* Yes, indeed!

Lily exits into the corridor

George *(collapsing)* Oh, my God!
Pamela *(laughing)* I thought we did rather well, George.

There is a knock on the door. George freezes

George She's come back for a second opinion.
Pamela *(calling)* Who is it?
Maria *(off)* It's the chambermaid.
Pamela ⎱*(together)* In the bathroom.
George ⎰

Richard enters 650 lounge from 650 bedroom with Jennifer who is wearing the wig
George exits into 648 bathroom and closes the door

Jennifer I'm not going without my sunglasses.
Richard I must have left them by the telephone next door.

Richard exits into the corridor, leaving the door open

Jennifer exits into 650 bedroom, closing the door, as:

Pamela opens 648 corridor door to:

Maria, the chambermaid, who steps into 648 lounge

Maria *(giggling)* Make bed now?

Pamela (*giggling*) I'm afraid not. It's in use off and on all afternoon. (*She pushes Maria out and closes the corridor door*)

Maria exits

(*Opening the bathroom door*) Quick!

George starts to come out of the bathroom as:

Pamela opens the corridor door

Richard is standing in the corridor outside 648, about to knock on the door

Pamela bangs the door in Richard's face

(*To George*) Richard!

George returns to 648 bathroom and closes the door

Pamela opens the corridor door

Richard enters 648 lounge

Pamela smiles sweetly at him

Richard Why did you slam the door like that?
Pamela (*after a moment's pause*) I thought it might amuse you.
Richard Nearly gave me a stroke.
Pamela Sorry. I thought you were going for a stroll.
Richard I am. I had to come back. For my sunglasses. (*He moves to the phone*)
Pamela Sunglasses?
Richard It's very bright in the corridor.

Pamela suddenly remembers that George has them and looks towards the bathroom door

(*Looking around*) Have you seen them, darling?
Pamela Yes.
Richard Good.
Pamela I threw them out of the bedroom window. (*She moves quickly towards the bedroom*)
Richard (*amazed*) Out of the . . .? What the dickens for?
Pamela Felt like it.
Richard Really! (*Suddenly*) I know! There's an old pair in my sponge bag. (*He moves towards the bathroom*)
Pamela (*stopping him*) No!

Richard stops

Richard Yes there is.
Pamela No. You prefer feminine ones, don't you?
Richard Yes, please. (*Quickly*) I mean . . .! Large ones *would* be better, yes. Keep more light out.
Pamela (*pushing him towards the bedroom*) There's a pair of mine in the bedroom. In my blue case.

Richard Thank you, darling.

Richard hurries into 648 bedroom, closing the door

Pamela (*opening 648 bathroom door*) Hurry!

George comes into 648 lounge. He is now properly dressed and carries his briefcase

(*Opening the corridor door*) You'll ask me to be Mrs Christmas again, won't you?

George Yes, in nineteen-ninety-five.

George hurries out into the corridor and closes the door

Richard hurries in from the bedroom with Pamela's sunglasses. He puts them on

Richard That's better.

Richard goes to open the corridor door but Pamela steps in to bar his way

Pamela (*vamping him*) You won't be long will you, Richard.

Richard No fear.

Pamela I haven't felt like this for ages.

Richard Neither have I!

Richard exits into the corridor and Pamela exits into 648 bedroom, both closing the doors behind them

At the same time, George enters 650 lounge from the corridor and knocks on the bedroom door

Jennifer appears from 650 bedroom, still without her jacket and carrying a glass of champagne

George Sunglasses.

Jennifer Where on earth have you been?!

George (*indicating his neck*) Up to here most of the time!

Jennifer gives George her champagne glass and puts the sunglasses on

Richard hurries into 650 lounge and closes the corridor door

Richard What's going on? Where the hell have you been, Pigden?

George (*shouting*) I'm doing my best for everybody!

Richard (*to Jennifer*) Right! Here's some sunglasses. (*He goes to give Jennifer Pamela's glasses but stops on seeing Jennifer wearing her original ones*) Where did you get these from?

Jennifer Mr Pigden just gave them to me.

Richard (*to George*) Pamela threw them out of the bedroom window.

George (*after a moment's pause*) I thought it was funny. I was walking out of the hotel just now to go back to the Home Office and I put my hand out to see if it was raining and Mrs Bristow's sunglasses landed right——

Richard (*interrupting*) Never mind! (*To Jennifer*) You'd better go, my sweet. (*He opens the corridor door*)

Jennifer I'll get my jacket.

Jennifer hurries into 650 bedroom

Lily comes out of room 649 opposite and sees Richard

Lily Richard!!

Lily comes in. Richard breaks away and looks to heaven. George turns and puts his face into the wall

Richard Oh, my God! (*Pleasantly*) Hello, Lily!
Lily (*to Richard*) What on earth are you doing here?
Richard I'm staying here, remember.
Lily But you're in that suite next door, aren't you?
Richard Ah!—yes. I'm *visiting* here.
Lily Visiting?
Richard Yes. This room is occupied by my PPS.

He indicates George who very clearly has his back to the situation. George is still holding Jennifer's champagne

I say!

George turns away even more

I say!!

George, still with his back to them, holds his glass up and scrutinizes the champagne

Say how do you do to *Mrs Chatterton.*

George takes a deep breath and turns. After a moment he emits his nervous giggle

Lily (*surprised*) Good heavens.

George goes to speak, can think of nothing to say so he turns his back on them once again and surveys his glass of champagne

Richard (*turning George around*) You can leave that now! Say hello to Mrs
    Chatterton!
Lily (*to Richard*) I don't quite understand. Did you say this gentleman is
    your PPS?
Richard Yes. Best PPS in the business.
Lily (*looking at George, confused*) PPS?
George Yes. PPS.
Lily (*to Richard*) He's your personal private secretary?
George No, I'm his personal physician and surgeon.

Lily frowns. Richard's face goes very blank

Richard (*finally*) Hang on a second ...
George I'm the best personal *physician* and *surgeon* in the business.
Richard (*madly thinking*) Physician—surgeon?

George (*to Lily*) I've just been giving Mr Willey his annual check-up. He's had a little injection and he's not quite with it.

Lily Oh. So you look after Mr Willey as well as his——

George (*interrupting quickly*) Yes! I look after Mr Willey as well as a lot of people. (*To Richard*) I'm a very busy physician, aren't I?

Richard (*trying to work it out*) Oh, yes!

George And I'm extremely pleased with your physical condition, Mr Willey. Yes. And—er—thanks for the specimen.

He hands Richard Jennifer's glass of champagne. Richard nonplussed, takes it. George smiles reassuringly at Lily who is looking somewhat bemused. Richard, at a loss, drinks the champagne in one gulp. Lily looks amazed at George

(*To Lily, finally*) It's an old Hindu custom. Well, if you'll excuse me, I think Dr Christmas ought to hit the trail for Norwich.

Jennifer comes out of 650 bedroom wearing the wig and sunglasses

Jennifer I'm ready to ... (*She stops on seeing Lily*)

George We'll take his blood pressure later, Sister. (*He pushes Jennifer back into the bedroom*)

Jennifer exits

(*Calling through into the bedroom*) And I've finished with the ultra-violet, so you can remove the protective goggles. (*He closes the bedroom door*)

Lily I think I'm in the way, Doctor.

George Well, I do have a very busy schedule.

Richard Yes, he's got several operations at St Thomas's. (*He opens the corridor door*)

Lily St Thomas's? (*To George*) I thought you practised in Norwich, Doctor.

George Yes, I do. I *practise* in Norwich but I actually *do* it at St Thomas's.

George politely pushes Lily out into the corridor. Richard closes the door

Lily exits

Richard What the hell were you playing at?

George *Playing?*

Richard You've never been introduced to her before, have you?

George (*innocently*) No.

Richard Bloody fool!

Jennifer enters from 650 bedroom

Give Pigden five minutes to check out, then you can go.

Jennifer OK.

Richard How long's your husband away skiing?

Jennifer Another ten days.

Richard Good. Pigden will call you in the morning with fresh hotel arrangements.

George No he won't!

Jennifer Invite your tea boy, Mr Pigden. We may get a reduction for groups.

Jennifer exits into 650 bedroom

Richard Right. You go and check out as Dr Christmas and then get back to the department. (*He opens the corridor door*)

George I suppose you'll be joining me now Mrs Bristow's had to be cancelled.

Richard I will *not* be joining you. I've got to spend the afternoon in bed with Mrs Willey.

George Have you?

Richard I don't know what's come over her but she's as randy as hell.

George hesitates and then gives a huge smirk. He then strolls innocently out through the corridor door and exits L

Richard, bemused, looks after him and then exits R along the corridor as:

The Waiter enters 648 lounge from the corridor

The Waiter looks around and then goes to knock on 648 bedroom door

Richard enters 648 lounge and sees the Waiter

(*Curtly*) Yes!?

Waiter Ahhh! (*In his surprise, he jumps round into his warlike kung-fu pose*)

Richard What do *you* want?

Waiter Me take trolley, champagne, caviare.

Richard We haven't finished with it.

Waiter You three pot coffee husband now?

Richard Yes!

Waiter You six-four-eight Willey?

Richard Yes!

Waiter All white men look alike.

The Waiter exits, shaking his head

Richard goes into 648 bedroom

Richard (*brightly*) Pamela!

The set changes to the hotel reception area

The table and chairs DR have been struck

The Receptionist and the Manager, who is working on some papers, are at the reception desk. Lily is in the phone kiosk

George hurries out of the lift and approaches the desk

Lily comes out of the phone kiosk nearly bumping into George

Lily You're in a hurry, Doctor.

George Yes, they've got an epidemic in Norwich.

Lily exits into the lift

George goes to the desk. The Receptionist reacts to it being George

Receptionist Oh. Yes, sir?
George I'd like to check out, please. I did ring down earlier. Dr Christmas, suite six-fifty.
Manager There we are, Doctor!

The Manager with a polite but steely smile, hands George the account

George (*surprised*) Oh.
Manager Where's Mrs Christmas?
George She's being dealt with. I mean—er—she's coming. Yes. Well, it's been a most enjoyable visit.
Manager (*still coldly*) Thank you.
George And it's been a marvellous rest!

The Manager reacts to the Receptionist

Done me the world of good.

During the ensuing dialogue, Edward enters through the revolving door and approches the desk. He is a tall, handsome young man in his twenties. He is dressed in a ski anorak and has his left foot bandaged and in a slipper. He walks with a stick

Manager I'm pleased to hear it.
George (*referring to his account*) Oh, I say. Cheap at the price. I'll pay cash.
Manager As you wish.

George takes a money clip from his pocket and starts to count the money

Edward (*to the Manager*) Excuse me.
Manager Yes, sir?
Edward Do you have somebody called Christmas staying in your hotel?
Manager (*warily*) Yes, sir, we do.
George (*looking up*) Christmas?
Edward *Doctor* Christmas?
Manager (*indicating George*) This is Dr Christmas.
Edward Great. I got your message.
George Message?
Edward (*leaning on his stick, taking an envelope from his pocket*) Yes.
George It's not from me, I'm sure ...

Edward takes a piece of notepaper from the envelope

Edward It's written on *Westminster Hotel* notepaper. (*Reading*) "Your phone out of order. Come immediately. Signed Dr Noel Christmas, suite six-fifty."

The Manager looks at George

George (*taking the note from Edward*) How did you get hold of this?
Edward You sent it to me, didn't you?
George To *you*?

Edward I'm Edward Bristow.
George (*blankly*) Edward Bristow?
Edward (*holding up the envelope*) Bristow, 34a Sloane Square.
George (*dumbly*) Bristow, 34a Sloane Square.
Edward It's rather fortunate I received it actually. I'm supposed to be on a skiing holiday—and yesterday, would you believe it? trying one of those crazy ski-jumps—sprained my bloody ankle.

George looks at the ankle, then looks back at Edward

Got back home this morning and found this on the table. So here I am!

George hesitates then looks blankly at Edward and at the Manager who has joined them in front of the desk. George can only emit his nervous laugh

You *did* want to see me, didn't you?
George (*at a loss*) Well, if your name's Bristow . . .
Edward Yes—although it doesn't actually say whether it's for *Mister* or *Missus* Bristow. (*He holds up the envelope*)
George (*in mock surprise*) Doesn't it?
Edward (*laughing*) Just Bristow.
George (*laughing*) Just Bristow.

George includes the Manager in the merriment. The Manager is not amused

Edward (*laughing*) Bit silly, really.
George (*laughing*) Bit silly.
Edward (*laughing*) Anyway, you sent the note——
George (*laughing*) I sent the note! (*Laughing, he slaps the Manager*)
Edward —so you can say whether it's for me or my wife.

George laughs profusely and then stops as he notices the Manager staring at him

George It's for *you*. Not your wife. I don't even know your wife. (*To the Manager*) Do you know his wife?

The Manager shakes his head

(*To Edward*) What did you say your wife's name was?
Edward Jennifer Bristow.
George Jennifer——

Jennifer alights from lift. She is wearing the wig and sunglasses

Bristow!!

Jennifer freezes for a fraction of a second. At the same time, George deftly kicks Edward's stick away from under him and Edward crashes to the floor

Jennifer gets back into the lift and departs

A very solicitous George and a worried Manager assist Edward to the chair DL, *the Manager having retrieved Edward's stick*

Dear, oh dear, oh dear.

Edward What the hell happened?
George It's these damned rugs in this hotel. (*To the Manager*) Somebody will break their neck one of these days. (*He pretends to slip*) Look at that!
Manager (*to Edward*) I'm most terribly sorry, sir.

The Manager moves to hand Edward his stick but George admonishingly grabs it from him

Edward No, it's OK. It was a bit sudden, that's all. I didn't even feel myself going.
George (*to Edward jokingly; handing him his stick*) It hasn't been your lucky week, has it?
Edward Too true.
George (*to the Manager*) You really should have non-slip carpets, you know.

The Manager glares at George. Edward stands up

Edward Look, Dr Christmas . . .
George Call me Noel, please.
Edward Noel. I wouldn't mind knowing what you wanted to see me for.
George (*blandly*) I can understand that.
Edward I was rather hoping it was an interview for a job, actually.
George A job, yes. Yes, it is! What do you do? I mean, what do you *prefer* to do?
Edward Well, theatre, I suppose.
George Theatre?
Edward Or television or film work.

The internal phone on the reception desk rings. The Manager answers it

I really don't mind what I do. I haven't been in the profession all that long.
George (*bemused*) Are you an actor?
Edward I imagined that's why you wanted to see me.
George (*brightly*) Yes.
Edward Well, is it about an acting job?
George (*brightly*) Yes!
Manager (*calling to George*) It's Mrs Christmas.
George (*startled, yelling*) Where?!

As he yells, George's reflex action makes him kick Edward's stick from under him once again. The stick goes flying and Edward crashes to the ground

At the same time the lift door opens and the Chinese Waiter comes out carrying a silver tray on which is a glass of brandy

George, in his panic, turns the Waiter round and pushes him back inside the lift. As George goes to assist Edward, the nervous Waiter re-appears with his tray and adopts a kung-fu pose. George sits Edward on a chair as the Manager indicates to the Waiter to get Edward's stick. The Waiter does so but keeps his distance

(*To Edward*) Dear, oh dear! You all right?

Edward I think so. It's funny. I just seem to go.

George You do, don't you? (*He pretends to slip*) That's the place. (*To the Manager*) Where were we?

The Manager holds out the phone

Manager (*impassively*) Your wife wishes to speak to you. From suite six-fifty.

George My wife. You mean the one with the red—er—and the—er—who I've just—er—yes! I've been expecting her to call down. (*On the phone*) Hello, darling, *Noel* here. Upstairs again now, are you? ... Yes, wasn't that a surprise? ... Yes, I bet you did, I nearly did, too! ... Well, I'm now of the opinion that we may need some help from the *Government*. I know *you* can't but I bloody well can! (*He replaces the receiver and smiles at the Manager*) That's for the swear box. (*He tips the Manager a coin. To Edward*) If you'll exuse me, there's a couple of people I need to see upstairs. (*To the Manager*) Too much polish everywhere, that's the trouble. (*He pretends to slip*) Look at that! Standing still and I nearly went. (*He "slips" again*) The whole place needs looking at.

George continues to slide. The Manager is standing there impassively. The Chinese Waiter is intrigued and comes closer to watch, leaning on Edward's stick. George finishes a slide to the left, a slide to the right and then kicks the stick from under the Waiter. The Waiter does a complete forward roll and comes up on his feet, still holding the tray and with the drink unspilled. (NB. This is a trick glass attached—but removable!—to the tray.) George removes the glass from the tray and drinks it. He leaves a distraught Waiter and a bemused Edward and Manager

George exits into the lift

The set changes to the bedroom and lounge of 648

Richard and Pamela are sitting up in bed drinking champagne. Neither looks very happy. The lounge is empty

Richard (*with false joviality*) Well, this is the life!

Pamela (*with equally false joviality*) Great, isn't it?

Richard Middle of the afternoon. I feel really—er—really ...

Pamela Sexy?

Richard That's the word, yes.

There is a pause

Mind you, there's no rush, is there? Got until about five o'clock to try to—to have a—have ...

Pamela Have another champagne, darling. (*She refills his glass*)

Richard Thank you. (*He drinks*)

Pamela (*refilling her own glass*) Yes, we should—er—do this more often.

Richard Yes. (*He suddenly laughs, the various pills and alcohol starting to take effect. The laughter becomes slightly strident*)

Pamela What are you laughing at?
Richard (*stopping laughing*) Nothing. I don't think I'd better have any more champagne, darling.
Pamela You feeling all right?
Richard You bet. Just the two of us—in bed—no distractions—relaxed!

The phone rings

Oh, my God!

They both look at the phone nervously and then smile at each other. Richard lifts the receiver

(*On the phone; gaily*) Hello? ... (*Worried*) George!
Pamela George?!
Richard (*to Pamela*) Sh! (*On the phone, gaily*) Everything all right?

There is a very short reply

(*Worried*) Oh!
Pamela Is it?
Richard Ssh! (*On the phone, gaily*) What are you doing back up there? What?!
Pamela Where is he?
Richard Ssh! (*On phone, gaily*) What are you doing back up there?
Pamela Back up where?
Richard Sssh! (*On the phone, with false joviality*) Well, come on, Pigden, it can't be as serious as all that. ... (*He listens for a moment, during which time his jovial face disintegrates into horror*) Oh, God help us all!
Pamela What's happened?

Richard jumps out of bed. He is wearing pyjama bottoms

Richard (*on the phone*) Stay there. I'll be with you as soon as I can. (*He bangs the phone down and hurries to the wardrobe to get his clothes*)
Pamela (*kneeling on the end of the bed*) What on earth is it?
Richard It's George. Hey, where's my blue suit?
Pamela You were wearing it at lunch time.
Richard I know, but where ... (*He stops as he realizes that he has left it in suite 650. He smiles broadly at Pamela*) Oh, yes! I—er—I gave it to the chambermaid to be cleaned. Blazer will do.

Both Richard and Pamela's minds are racing. During the ensuing scene Richard gets dressed, putting trousers over his pyjama bottoms

Pamela You were telling me about George. What on earth is it?
Richard I've got to go and see him.
Pamela Have you? Why?
Richard He's got himself into a bit of a pickle.
Pamela George has?
Richard A rather unpleasant one.
Pamela Shall I come with you?
Richard Oh, no! There's—er—somebody else involved.

Pamela (*worried*) Oh, yes?
Richard Yes.
Pamela (*apprehensively*) Who?
Richard Well, I—er—hate to tell you but—er—George is having an affair.
Pamela (*faintly*) Is he?
Richard Yes—with a gay gentleman called Ted.

Pamela's mind does a somersault as she sits there with her mouth open

You're knocked sideways, aren't you?

Pamela nods

Well, it's even worse.
Pamela Is it?
Richard Ted's a tea boy from the Foreign Office.

Pamela blinks

Pamela I don't quite understand.
Richard While we were out, George and Ted have been using our suite.
Pamela (*after a pause, tentatively*) Ye-es.
Richard I practically caught them in our bathroom.
Pamela Ye-es.
Richard I'd better go and deal with Pigden and—er—Ted.
Pamela Where exactly *are* Pigden and—er—Ted?
Richard Er—I suppose it's safe to tell you. I suppose I'll have to tell you.
Pamela Ye-es?
Richard When they realized that they couldn't use our suite any more—do you know what they did?
Pamela No-o.
Richard They booked into the suite next door.
Pamela (*bemused*) And George is next door with Ted.
Richard (*with mock outrage*) Pretty staggering, isn't it?
Pamela (*after a pause*) Ye-es.

Richard is now dressed

Richard I'll be back as soon as I've sorted them out.
Pamela (*getting off the bed*) Richard! What exactly is the problem?
Richard Ah. Attempted suicide. (*He moves towards the lounge*)
Pamela What?! (*She grabs him*)
Richard Not George. Ted. He jumped out of the window.
Pamela (*totally bemused*) Ted did?!
Richard It's all right, he landed on the balcony.
Pamela (*very confused*) Richard, there must be some misunderstanding.
Richard There was. Apparently Ted caught George cuddling that Chinese waiter.
Pamela What?!

Richard hurries through into the lounge

Richard!

She hurries through into the lounge where Richard has opened the door into the corridor

Richard, I'm positive there's an explanation. Maybe George is having a nervous breakdown.

Richard Could be. Obviously a hell of a strain having an affair with a tea boy and a waiter at the same time.

Pamela Yes.

Richard And we don't know who else he may have been carrying on with.

Pamela No.

He pushes her into 648 bedroom and closes the door. She leans against the bedroom door

The Waiter enters 648 lounge from the corridor

Pamela stands in the bedroom, madly thinking

Richard (*tersely*) What do you want?

Waiter (*moving to the trolley*) I take trolley now.

Richard Come back later.

Waiter Why you here again?

Richard I live here.

Waiter You no Easter with Christmas?

Richard Go away!

Waiter Me speak manager again.

Richard (*shouting*) Me get you sack!

Waiter (*yelling*) Ah!

The Waiter adopts a karate pose. Pamela enters the lounge from the bedroom

Pamela Anything wrong, darling?

Richard No, no.

Waiter (*to Pamela*) He your three pot coffee husband?

Richard Yes!

Waiter I speak Mrs Willey.

Richard (*hurrying to Pamela*) Well, Mrs Willey, doesn't want to speak to you, it's all his fault, isn't it, darling?

Pamela What? Oh! Yes!

Waiter What my fault?

Richard The mess next door.

Waiter Mess?

Richard Yes. With degenerates like you around, no wonder everybody's trying hari-kari.

Waiter Harry who?

Richard Leave it to me, Pamela. And don't come next door whatever you do. It's a ghastly sight. Blood everywhere.

Pamela Blood?

Waiter Blood?

Richard (*to Pamela*) Yes, didn't I tell you. When he wasn't able to jump, poor Ted tried to . . . (*He mimes cutting his throat and then pushes Pamela into the bedroom, closing the door*)

Waiter (*to Richard*) Blood, next door?

Richard Yes, bloody blood! (*He emits his foolish laugh*)

Waiter Bloody blood?

Richard Bloody well shove off.

Richard hurries into the corridor

Waiter He no talk me like that!

The Waiter goes through a series of furious karate blows on an imaginary assailant finally striking the trolley and hurting his hand

The Waiter pushes the trolley into the corridor as:

The set changes to become the lounge and bedroom of Suite 650

650 lounge goes to R and 650 bedroom to L. The bedroom has a window in the L wall and has similar furniture to that in 648. Please see ground plan D on page 92

An agitated George and resigned Jennifer are in the lounge of 650. Jennifer's wig and sunglasses are on the chair in the lounge. The trolley is still in the bedroom from Act I. George is speaking on the phone and his ensuing speech covers the set change

George (*on the phone*) No, it's no good Mr Bristow waiting at reception. You tell him I'll see him at my surgery in Norwich. . . . I'll check out when you've got rid of Mr Bristow! (*He puts the phone down*)

Jennifer Edward won't go if he thinks you've got an acting part for him. Poor sweetheart's been out of work for ages.

George Well, Mr Willey can explain why a personal private secretary to a government minister is posing as a family doctor from Norwich who's auditioning an out-of-work actor from Sloane Square.

Richard hurries into 650 lounge from the corridor

Richard (*to Jennifer*) You poor girl, you must have got a dreadful shock seeing your husband at reception like that.

Jennifer Mr Willey, I've got to get out of here, you've got to get back to your wife and Mr Pigden's got to get rid of my husband.

George What?

Richard Yes. (*Pulling George DR*) And if Pamela mentions it, Ted jumped out of the window——

George What?!

Richard —because he caught you cuddling the Chinese waiter.

George What?!

The Waiter enters 650 lounge from the corridor, leaving the door open

Waiter Excuse please.

Richard Oh, my God!

Waiter (*to Richard*) You *here* now.

Richard Yes!
Waiter Where blood?
George Blood?

The Waiter looks for blood on the carpet. So does George

Waiter He say blood in here.
Richard I'll say a bloody sight more in here if you don't clear off!
Jennifer Steady! Please, Dickie darling.
Waiter You Dickie darling now!
Richard Go away!
Waiter Me told six-fifty checking out.
Richard Buzz off!
Waiter You no talk me like that.
Richard Me talk you how me bloody want.
Jennifer Darling!
Waiter Me speak manager again.
George No, no please. He bit distressed.
Richard So I should think. Me give him twenty quid and he land me in it up
    to here.
Waiter Me do what?
Richard You flung dung!
Waiter I no Flung Dung, me Wong!
Richard Too bloody white, you wong.
George Charlie upset.
Waiter Charlie? He Dickie!
Richard And feeling worse all the time. You push off to Peking.
Waiter Me take you race relations board.
George Oh, my God!
Richard You take me anywhere you bloody want.
Waiter You reason British lost Commonwealth!
Richard Bloody good riddance too!
Jennifer Dickie!
Waiter Dickie not in India now.
Richard And "Who Flung Dung" not in bloody Hong Kong!
Waiter Up your London Bridge!
Richard And up your Khyber Pass!
Waiter Ah!

The Waiter takes his arm back to deliver a blow at Richard but hits George,
who collapses to his knees. Richard hurries to assist George to his feet as:

> *Lily comes out of her room opposite and pops her head through the open*
> *door*

Lily Oh, I say ... (*She sees Jennifer*) Oh! I know you, don't I?

Richard and George exchange a glance

Jennifer (*brightly*) I don't think so. (*She picks up her wig and sunglasses and*
    goes into 650 bedroom, closing the door behind her. During the following
    dialogue she listens at the door)

Lily (*seeing George*) I thought there was an epidemic in Norwich, Doctor.
George It was a false alarm.
Lily Oh, so you're having a party now, are you?
George No. Demonstrating yoga. (*To the Waiter*) Very good.

The Waiter is bemused

Richard (*to the Waiter, very sweetly*) Thank you, my good man, you may
go. (*He gives him a £20 tip*)
Waiter (*to Richard, smiling*) Still good place for British diplomacy.
Richard (*to the Waiter, smiling*) And even better place for Chinese cracker.
Waiter (*politely*) Ah, so.

The Waiter bows and exits, closing the corridor door behind him

Lily Of course! That young lady, she's one of the PM's little secretaries.

Richard and George look aghast at each other

Richard Yes! She's called to see the doctor.
Lily (*surprised*) Dr Christmas?
George Yes.
Richard Yes. He's her gynaecologist.
George Oh, my God! (*He walks away*)
Lily (*to George*) Oh. Has she had a little surprise?
George She certainly has.
Lily She's got a husband, I hope.
George Yes, he'll be even more surprised.
Richard I suggest you escort Mrs Bristow out of the hotel, Doctor.
George But we might bump——
Richard Right away, Doctor.

There is a knock at the door

George (*calling out*) Who is it?
Manager (*off*) It's the manager.

Richard and George exchange a glance

George (*calling*) Are you by yourself?
Manager (*off*) Open the door, please!
Richard (*to George*) Leave the manager to me. You look after Mrs Bristow.
Finish your pregnancy test.
George Yes. (*To Lily*) If you're ever in Norwich, I'll do the same for you.

*Lily reacts as George hurries into 650 bedroom. As George locks the bedroom
door from the inside Jennifer joins him and they stand by the door straining to
hear what's going on in the lounge. At the same time Richard opens the
corridor door*

The Manager storms into 650 lounge

Manager Dr Christmas, you should have checked out ... (*He stops on
seeing Richard*) Mr Willey!

Richard Are you by yourself?
Manager (*surprised*) Yes.
Richard Good, keep it up!

Richard laughs hysterically. The Manager looks nervous. Richard suddenly "wipes" his laugh. This makes the Manager more nervous

(*To Lily*) Nice to have chatted to you, Lily. I'll see you in the Commons tonight. (*He indicates for her to leave*)
Lily You will that. (*To the Manager, joking, but with a straight face*) If it's a boy, we'll call it Big Ben.

Lily exits leaving the Manager bemused. She closes the door behind her

Manager (*to Richard*) Where's Dr Christmas?
Richard He's in the bedroom (*loudly for George's benefit*) examining his wife.

The Manager glares at Richard and goes to open the bedroom door. It is locked

Manager (*knocking on the door*) Open this door!
George I can't. My wife's stark naked and I've got my hands full.
Manager (*to Richard*) God knows why they put up with him in Norwich.
Richard No. You leave him to me.
Manager (*firmly*) I'd much prefer that you return to your room, Mr Willey.
Richard I've locked myself out.
Manager (*coldly*) Then I shall let you in. (*He takes out his bunch of keys*)
Richard (*beaming*) What a very good idea. (*Shouting across the Manager to George*) Goodbye, Doctor! I'm off now! So is the manager *for a moment!*
Manager We'll all be deaf in a minute. (*He moves away from the bedroom door*) After you, Mr Willey. (*He opens the door into the corridor*)

Pamela comes into 650 lounge from the corridor

George and Jennifer are glued to the bedroom door trying to listen

Pamela Richard, is everything——?

Richard hastily takes her DR

Richard (*quickly*) Darling, I told you to stay in your room.
Pamela You've been so long. I was wondering if everything was all right.

Richard suddenly emits his laugh and then "wipes" immediately. The Manager takes a pace back towards the bedroom door where he remains

Where's George?
Manager George?
George (*calling*) Yes?
Richard (*across the Manager*) Shut up!
Manager Who's George, for heaven's sake?
Pamela (*to Richard*) Has anything happened to George?
Richard Not yet, but stick around.

Pamela And did you sort it out with Ted?

Richard Don't worry about Ted. (*To the Manager*) She's worried about Ted.

Manager (*po-faced*) Is she?

Richard Yes. *You've* heard about *Ted.*

Manager Yes, but it's the first I've heard about *George.*

George (*calling*) Yes?

Richard (*across the Manager*) Shut up! (*To the Manager*) George is sort of involved with Ted.

Manager And what about the doctor?

Pamela Doctor?

Manager Dr Christmas!

George (*calling*) Yes?!

Richard (*across the Manager*) Shut up!

George is getting frustrated and confused. So is the Manager

(*Quickly*) My wife knows nothing about Dr Christmas, do you, darling?

Pamela (*hastily*) No, I know nothing about Dr Christmas.

Manager Well, your husband does.

Pamela (*worried*) Does he?

Manager And about Mrs Christmas.

Pamela (*more worried*) Mrs Christmas?

Richard My wife doesn't want to know anything about Mrs Christmas.

Manager She's a nymphomaniac.

Pamela (*even more worried*) Mrs Christmas is a nymphomaniac?

Manager She attacked Mr Willey.

Pamela (*confused*) Mrs Christmas did?

Richard (*to Pamela*) It's all tied up with the tea boy from the FO.

Manager (*flatly*) The tea boy from the FO.

Pamela (*to the Manager*) Have *you* met the tea boy from the FO?

Manager God knows *who* I've met!

George Is it safe to come out?

Manager ⎱
Richard ⎰ (*together*) Shut up!

Richard emits his brief laugh, stops and turns to the surprised Manager

Manager Now listen. I'd like to know more about this tea boy.

Richard Really? I'll put you in touch.

The Manager looks blank

Manager And where Ted and Charlie fit in.

Pamela *Charlie?*

Richard Charlie's another of George's darlings.

Pamela I simply can't believe it of George.

Manager (*shouting*) What's George got to do with all this?!

George (*yelling*) Nothing!

Manager I've had enough of this. (*Shouting at the door*) Come out!

He bangs the door. George has his ear close to it and gets his head jarred

George (*calling*) I didn't quite catch that.
Manager (*to the door*) I am not leaving until this door is opened.

In the bedroom, George and Jennifer exchange a terrified glance. During the following dialogue George lifts the table-cloth on the trolley and indicates for Jennifer to get on the lower shelf. She does so but only after some assistance from George as it is a very tight squeeze. George hands her the wig and sunglasses and pulls the table-cloth down, over the side of the trolley

George Still can't hear you.
Manager (*shouting*) I am staying here until you open this door.
George (*calling*) Beginning to filter through now.
Manager (*shouting louder*) Come out or I'll call the security officer.
George (*calling*) Yes. I'm receiving you loud and clear. One more time. (*He has hidden Jennifer and unlocks the door*)
Manager (*shouting louder*) Come out or I'll call——
George (*opening the door*) No need to shout. (*He comes into the lounge wheeling the trolley*)
Manager I'm glad you've decided to be sensible, Doctor.
George Of course.
Manager Where's Mrs Christmas?
George On the window ledge.
Manager }
Pamela } (*together*) What?!
George I think she's going to jump.

There is a fractional pause then:

Pamela (*rushing to the bedroom window*) Oh, my God!
Manager (*rushing to the bedroom window*) I hope we're in time! Don't panic her.

During the above two lines George quickly pulls up the table-cloth to reveal to Richard where Jennifer is. Richard gives him the thumbs up sign and hurries to join Pamela and the Manager

Richard (*moving to the bedroom window*) Where is she?! Where is she?!

George quickly locks the bedroom door and puts the key in his pocket

George (*to Jennifer*) Quick! Out you get!
Jennifer God, I'm stuck!
George Oh, no!

They try to dislodge her but she is firmly wedged. George tries to shove her from the rear

Jennifer (*yelling*) Ah!
George Ssh! (*He continues to struggle with her*)

In the bedroom the Manager, Richard and Pamela have been leaning out of the window looking for Mrs Christmas

Manager (*turning away from the window*) I thought as much. If she'd jumped we'd have seen her body.

Richard (*stalling for time*) Wind may have carried her round the corner.

The Manager glares at him

Manager Excuse me! (*He pushes past Richard and goes to open the door but finds it locked. Calling*) Dr Christmas!

George is still trying to release Jennifer

George (*calling*) He's gone. (*To Jennifer, whispering*) It's no good. Let's go and find the fire escape.

Manager Open this door.

George opens the corridor door

George (*sweetly calling to the bedroom door*) Coming! (*He looks into corridor and immediately slams the door shut*) Oh, my God!

Jennifer What is it?

George Your husband!

Jennifer My husband?!

George Getting out of the lift. (*He opens 650 bathroom door*)

Manager (*banging on the bedroom door*) Dr Christmas! Open this door please!

Richard I told you he had a mania for locking people away.

Manager One of my pass keys will fit.

Richard (*loudly for George's benefit*) One of his pass keys will fit!

The Manager reacts to Richard yelling. During the next few lines George pushes the trolley into the bathroom and the Manager tries one or two keys in the bedroom door

George (*to Jennifer*) I'll deal with your husband. Don't move till I get back.

Jennifer I can't.

George (*without thinking*) Pour yourself a bowl of water.

   George shuts the bathroom door and hurries out into the corridor

The Manager finds the correct key

Manager (*entering the lounge*) Doctor, I demand ...

Richard and Pamela follow him in

Richard (*pleased*) All clear! (*Quickly*) I mean, nobody here!

Manager I'll check at reception. Will both of you wait in your suite, please.

During the following, the set changes

Richard No. (*To Pamela*) You go and keep the bed warm, darling. I'll accompany the manager in case Dr Christmas turns funny. (*To the Manager*) Turns funny! (*He does a pirouette to demonstrate "turning funny" and at the same time laughs hysterically. Still laughing, to the Manager*) After you!

Richard indicates for the Manager to exit but instead Richard himself marches out laughing into the corridor and exits L

The Manager looks at Pamela who smiles weakly

With a hopeless shrug the Manager goes out into the corridor and exits L

Pamela hesitates then exits into the corridor and moves off R, *closing the door behind her, as:*

George ushers Edward into 648 lounge from the corridor

The set has now become the lounges of suites 648 and 650. 650 lounge has moved to L *and 648 lounge is* R

George Wasn't that a bit of luck bumping into you like that up here.
Edward Well, I got fed up with waiting downstairs—hey, I thought you were in suite six-fifty, Doctor.
George This is mine as well. Sort of waiting room. You sit here and relax while I check if it's all clear in six-fifty.

George sits Edward by the phone

Edward I'd rather know about this acting job you're seeing me for.
George I'll be back in about two minutes.
Edward Couldn't you tell me something about the part?
George Very big! (*He opens the corridor door to go out*)

But Pamela hurries in

Pamela George, what in heaven—oh. (*She stops on seeing Edward*)
George (*indicating Edward*) This—is a young friend of mine.
Edward (*to Pamela*) Pleased to meet you.
George (*to Pamela*) He's not staying long.
Pamela (*nonplussed*) How do you do.
Edward (*offering his hand*) The name's Bristow. Edward Bristow.

Pamela goes to put her hand out

    Most of my chums call me Ted.

Pamela's hand stops in mid-air as the implication hits her. George puts his hand to his head and walks away DR *in mortified disbelief*

Pamela (*finally*) Ted.
George I don't think we need stay, Ted.
Edward Good, we're going next door now are we.
Pamela (*furious*) Oh!
Edward (*to Pamela*) Will you excuse me?
Pamela (*angrily*) No I won't!
George (*trying to laugh*) She won't!
Edward Beg your pardon?
Pamela (*to George*) And I thought Ted was made up for my benefit.
Edward No, it's the Italian sun-tan that does it.

Pamela looks bemused. George tries to laugh it off again

George Stop kidding, Ted.
Pamela I don't know what to say, George.
Edward George?
George Most of my chums call me George.
Edward You said Noel.
George Yes. Well there is no "L" in George.

George looks pleased with his explanation as Pamela and Edward work it out

Pamela (*to George*) I must say Ted's recovered remarkably quickly.
Edward Recovered?
Pamela I heard all about you trying to jump.

Edward thinks she must be talking about the skiiing. He holds out his foot

Edward Oh, well, you've got to have a go, haven't you?
Pamela (*distressed*) Oh!
Edward (*chuckling*) I didn't quite kill myself anyway.
Pamela It's not funny! And to have another attempt was absolutely wicked.
Edward Well, it was a very difficult jump.
George I'm sure it was.
Pamela Young man, you have so much to look forward to.
Edward Yeah. I'll probably have another go next winter and take a couple of friends with me.
Pamela Please, no!
George Come on, Ted. (*To Pamela*) I'll take him next door to finish off.
Pamela George!
George I mean ... (*To Ted*) Say goodbye, Ted.
Edward Oh. Nice to have met you—Mrs Willey, was it?
George Yes. Say "goodbye to Mrs Willey Wassit". (*He pushes Edward out into the corridor*)

Edward exits

Things aren't what they seem, Mrs Willey.
Pamela You're telling me. I'm shattered, George.
George Shattered? I'm practically demolished.

George hurries out into the corridor

Pamela slams the corridor door, bursts into tears and runs into 648 bedroom as:

The bathroom door of 650 opens and Jennifer, still stuck in the trolley, paddles it into the lounge. All that can be seen of her are her arms

George unlocks the corridor door of 650 and comes in

(*As he enters*) This way, Mr Bristow——(*He sees the moving trolley*)

Edward enters 650 from the corridor

George immediately about turns Edward and pushes him out into the corridor

—that way, Mr Bristow! (*He quickly pushes the trolley back into the bathroom*)

There is a loud crash from off as the trolley hits the unseen sink and medicine chest. Edward walks back in from the corridor, looking bemused. George hastily slams the bathroom door. He smiles happily at Edward as the loud glass crashes continue, caused by Jennifer and the trolley running amok in the bathroom. George finally opens the bathroom door a couple of inches

(*Calling into the bathroom*) You naughty pussy! (*He closes the bathroom door. To Edward*) She's got a mouse in there. (*He opens the bathroom door*) Drop it! (*He closes the bathroom door and moves Edward away*) She understands every word I say. I take her everywhere with me.

Edward Look, Dr Christmas . . .
George George.
Edward George. I'd like to know what this is all about.
George Of course.
Edward I mean, it is some kind of audition, isn't it?
George Yes. It's to do with a very nice part in a very nice film I'm making.
Edward Film?
George Yes. Film. Now, you may be wondering what a Norwich doctor is doing making a film . . .
Edward I was rather.
George Yes. I'm making it for the British Medical Association.
Edward I see.
George Norfolk Division.
Edward It all sounds very interesting.

There is another loud glass crash from the bathroom

George She's caught another one. Look, I think I'd rather audition you in the bedroom. (*He moves to the bedroom door and opens it*)
Edward Bedroom?
George Didn't I tell you? The entire action of the film takes place in bed.
Edward In bed?
George It's all about a young couple and their marital problems.
Edward Wait a minute, if it's one of these explicit sex movies . . .
George (*outraged*) Explicit sex? It's for showing in schools.
Edward (*weakening*) Well, what's this film called?
George *A Bit of the Other.*

Edward looks perplexed

Edward That's a funny title.
George It's a funny film. (*He pushes Edward into the bedroom*) Take your clothes off and get into bed. Think yourself into the part. Think of all the problems you've got with your wife. (*He closes the door. Taking the key from his pocket and locking the door*) And I'll think of all the problems I've got with *everybody's* wife. (*He opens 650 bathroom door and pulls the trolley out*)

Richard hurries into 648 lounge from the corridor

Richard Pamela! Pamela!

Richard goes into 648 bedroom, closing the door

George (*bending down to Jennifer and lifting the cloth*) I'm terribly sorry, Mrs Bristow.
Jennifer I'm still absolutely stuck.
George Let's get you out of *here* anyway. (*He opens the corridor door*)

Maria, the chambermaid, enters

Maria Scusa!
George Yes, *si, si*? (*He realizes that Jennifer is visible*) No, see see. (*He pulls the table-cloth down to hide Jennifer*)
Maria I turn bed down?
George No. You'll have to come back much later, thank you.
Maria I do nothing with beds today.
George You're in good company. Could you tell me where the fire escape stairs are please?
Maria Is there fire, señor?
George No, but plenty smoke.

George pushes the trolley into the corridor and exits R. *Maria follows him, leaving the door ajar*

Pamela and Richard come into 648 lounge from 648 bedroom. Pamela is crying. Richard is patting her consolingly and chuckling at the same time

Richard Now, now! Not serious. Pigden is gay, that's all. I'll probably be able to hush it up.

Pamela cries

After all, it doesn't actually affect you, does it?
Pamela (*tearfully*) He was always so sweet and gentle. To think he's had Ted with him all the time.

Richard sits her

Richard I'm as surprised as you are. They must have been at it in the Foreign Office, too.

Pamela cries

There, there. I'll order a pot of tea. (*He lifts the phone and dials*)
Pamela But they were both so blatant about it just now.
Richard Well, they've decided to leave the closet. (*On the phone*) A pot of tea in six-four-eight, please. . . . No, *not* six cups and don't be so bloody funny!
Pamela (*sniffing*) And George actually saying to my face he was going next door to finish it off with Ted.
Richard (*on the phone*) You'd better send up a bottle of brandy, too. (*He replaces the receiver*) Well, as much as I don't wish to interrupt I'd better

go and make sure George leaves before the manager has the police up here.

Pamela Well, you be careful of Ted. He's obviously unbalanced. I mean he looks perfectly normal but he and his friends are planning a mass suicide next winter.

Richard (*after trying to take this in*) Excuse me, darling. (*He moves to the door*)

Pamela Richard?

Richard Yes, dear.

Pamela You know this Mrs Christmas who was next door?

Richard Ye-es.

Pamela The one who's a nymphomaniac.

Richard Ye-es.

Pamela I've been thinking about her.

Richard I wouldn't do that, darling.

Pamela Do you know what I reckon?

Richard No.

Pamela I reckon it's Ted and he's a transvestite.

Richard It's not a bad idea, darling.

Pamela And, Richard! There's George's other friend to fit in somewhere.

During the following the set changes

Richard You mean, the waiter?

Pamela No, Charlie.

Richard Yes. George has obviously got them on shiftwork.

Richard emits his foolish laugh and exits into the corridor

Pamela cries to herself

The set has now become the lounge and bedroom of Suite 650. 650 lounge has moved R and 650 bedroom is L. The lounge is empty. Edward is sitting up in bed in the bedroom. He has undressed and is now wearing pants and socks. The remainder of his clothes are on the suitcase rack along with his stick. After a moment he gets out of bed and picks up his stick. He goes to open the door but discovers it's locked. He bangs on the door

Edward Hey! George!

Richard enters 650 lounge, from the corridor, and closes the door

Richard George! (*Opening the bathroom door and calling in*) George!

There is more banging from the bedroom. Richard closes the bathroom door and turns

Edward Hey!

Richard reacts and moves to the bedroom door. He unlocks it

(*As the door opens*) What's the idea? (*He stops on seeing Richard*)

Richard (*pushing past Edward into the bedroom*) Where's George?

Edward That's what I was wondering. I've been in bed waiting for him.

Richard, who has been looking under the bed, stops and looks slowly round at Edward. For the first time Richard takes in Edward's state of undress

Richard Oh! I suppose *you're* Ted, are you?
Edward Yes.
Richard Well, I hope you're satisfied.
Edward I can't say I am. Wait minute, I recognize you, don't I?
Richard (*tersely*) Willey!
Edward Of course, Willie Whitelaw!
Richard Richard Willey!
Edward Sorry, yes. I've seen you on *Panorama* and things.
Richard (*sternly*) Have you?
Edward Very pleased to meet you, sir. (*He holds out his hand*)
Richard (*surprised*) Oh. How do you do.

Edward shakes hands warmly

Edward Are you a friend of George's?
Richard I *work* with George.
Edward (*surprised*) Oh. (*Chuckling*) Well, I can't believe he's got you and me here for the same thing.
Richard Certainly not. I know what *you're* here for.
Edward Do you?
Richard Yes!
Edward George says it's called *A Bit of the Other*.
Richard (*outraged*) Good God! All right! You can go now.
Edward No fear. George wants to see what I'm like in bed first.

Edward moves down a pace and Richard sees Edward's bandaged foot

Richard (*coldly*) How did you do that?
Edward Oh. Trying something tricky and my bindings broke.

Richard tries to work out what he thinks is some reference to chains and bondage

Richard You're outrageous!
Edward Let's call it quietly confident.
Richard Let's call it bloody cock-sure!

Richard thrusts Edward's trousers at him and strides angrily into the lounge. Edward follows him, holding the trousers, and crosses to the chair where he leaves them

Edward What the hell are you getting so upset about? We all have to start somewhere. This film could do me a lot of good.

Richard hesitates

Richard Film? What film?
Edward The one George is making.

Richard looks around for the hidden camera. He then returns to the bedroom to see if there is a camera above the bed. Richard returns to the lounge, still searching

Richard He doesn't go in for *that* kind of thing, does he?!
Edward That's why I'm here, Mr Willey. Wait a minute—"Willey". That must have been your wife I met next door—Mrs Willey.
Richard Yes it was and she's very upset about what you're doing with George.
Edward Why, does she want to be in the film too?
Richard Certainly not!

George enters 650 lounge in a very agitated condition, closing the door behind him. He goes straight to the bedroom door, looks in, sees the bedroom empty and then closes the door

George Oh dear. (*He sees Richard and Edward*) Oh dear!
Richard I don't know what to say to you, Pigden.
Edward Pigden?
Richard (*to Edward*) You keep quiet, you treacherous tea boy!
Edward Tea boy?
George Ohh! Mr Willey, I need to tell you something!
Richard I've heard quite enough, you pornographic poofter, Pigden!
Edward Pigden?
Richard (*to Edward*) You get dressed, you little tea bag! (*He laughs hysterically at his joke and suddenly stops*)
Edward I think Mr Willey's got a screw loose.
Richard And you're the expert on screws!
Edward Now, wait a——!
George (*to Edward, but for Richard's benefit*) Please, *Mr Bristow*! Mr Willey's been through a lot today, *Mr Bristow*.
Richard You don't have to make excuses ... You called him Bristow.
George Yes.
Richard (*to Edward*) Is your name Bristow?
Edward Yes. Edward Bristow.
George Yes. Husband of Jennifer. Aren't you, Ted?

George puts his arm round Edward's shoulder. There is a pause as Richard takes it in

Richard (*still dazed*) Jennifer is married to a queer tea boy. (*He sits, bemused, by the telephone table*)
George Oh God! (*He goes and leans on the back wall, weeping*)
Edward (*to George*) Why the devil does he think I'm a queer tea boy?

George turns round with a maniacal gleam in his eye

George Because that's one of the parts in the film I'm making! Mr Willey wants to play it. He's leaving politics and taking up dramatic art. And now he's upset because he thinks I'm offering the queer tea boy to *you* and I'm not, because you're the *husband*. (*To Richard*) *Forget* the queer tea boy, that's your part. You've got it.

Edward Oh, I see. I think you'd be quite good as a queer tea boy.
Richard (*in a daze*) Could we have a recap please?
George In a minute. (*To Edward*) If you'd kindly wait in the bathroom.
Edward Bathroom?
George I'd like to see how you look in the bath now.

    Edward is pushed into the bathroom by George

Richard I've never met such a kinky pair.
George (*closing the bathroom door*) Never mind him. I've lost Mrs Bristow.
Richard (*rising*) Lost her?
George She was jammed in the trolley, remember?
Richard Of course I remember.
George Well I put the trolley in the lift.
Richard Yes?
George And the lift and the trolley went before I could get in.
Richard Bloody fool! Go and find her.

    Edward enters from the bathroom

Edward George—do we need water in the bath?
George No.
Edward Well, what are we waiting for then?

There is a knock on the corridor door

George Who is it?
Manager (*off*) The manager.
George The manager!

    Edward is pushed into the bathroom by George

George closes the bathroom door and sits nonchalantly. Richard opens the corridor door

    The Manager storms in

Manager Dr Christmas—I . . . (*He stops on seeing Richard*) Mr Willey!
Richard (*jovially*) Good-afternoon!
Manager Why do I keep finding you here?
Richard Just lucky, I suppose. (*He emits his laugh*)
Manager There's nothing to laugh at!
Richard (*stopping laughing*) Who's laughing? Now, you're probably worried about this maniac here. (*He indicates George*)
Manager Among others.
Richard And you possibly want to know how the young lady came to be stuck in that position.
Manager (*bewildered*) What young lady in what position?
Richard The young lady under your . . . didn't you look under your . . .
Manager Under my what?!
Richard Nothing. Only if you had seen anyone it was only Mrs Christmas.
Manager Now look! I don't care if Dr and Mrs Christmas are the kindest

couple in Norwich—there's far too much sex in this hotel and I'm not having any of it!

Richard takes this in

Richard The doctor's prepared to go, sir, but he seems to have mislaid his wife.

Richard moves the Manager to the corridor door

The bathroom door opens and Edward appears. He is still in his underpants and carrying his stick

Edward (*entering*) Now look *here*——!

Before he can get any more out George grabs the stick, pushes Edward back into the bathroom and closes the door. The Manager, with his back to the proceedings, grabs Richard in fright but sees nothing of Edward

George (*singing and pushing Edward*) "*Here* we are again. Happy as can be. All good pals and jolly good company."

Edward exits into the bathroom

The Manager turns to look at George. During the above, George, using the stick as a cane, gives a passable performance of a seaside entertainer for the benefit of the Manager. Dazed, the Manager watches George who goes into a second chorus

(*Singing*) "Here we are again. Happy as can be. (*For Edward's benefit*) Put your clothes on very quick-er-ly."

The Manager looks at Richard who is smiling appreciatively. Richard applauds

Richard Jolly good, Doctor, jolly good. (*To the Manager*) He's practising for the medical convention cabaret.

George quickly locks the bathroom door while Richard has the Manager's attention

Manager It would help matters, Mr Willey, if you returned to your room.

There are three quick knocks on the bathroom door from Edward. The Manager turns and George, who is standing by the door, smiles at the Manager and then bangs the floor three times with his stick by way of explanation

(*To Richard*) Mr Willey, will you, please go back ...

There are more staccato knocks on the bathroom door from Edward. The Manager quickly turns. George goes into a brief tap dance

Richard (*to the Manager*) You're right. Let's go next door.
Manager (*to Richard*) Oh, no, I'm not leaving Dr Christmas.

There is more urgent knocking from Edward. The Manager turns furiously to look at George. George goes into a Spanish heel-tapping routine

George *Olé.*

The Manager manages to control himself. Richard applauds again

Richard Most impressive, Doctor.
Edward (*off*) Hey!
George (*quickly*) Hey!

George, on his haunches, does a hasty Russian step. He finally collapses against the wall. The Manager looks slowly at Richard who smiles at him

Richard It's the Norfolk air.
Edward (*off, shouting*) Will—somebody—let—me—out—of—here!

As Edward starts to call the Manager quickly turns. George immediately starts to vocally mime to Edward's voice. When Edward finishes George indicates to the Manager that he (George) is very adept at throwing his voice. George smiles at the Manager. The Manager looks at Richard who indicates how difficult is the art of throwing one's voice. The Manager advances on George who smiles

   (*Off, yelling*) Open this door!

George has no time to do anything and, as the Manager is looking directly at him, the game is up

Manager Ah! (*To Richard*) He's got a man locked in the bathroom.
Richard My God, he's at it again.

The Manager grabs the stick from George

Manager (*to George, strongly*) Sit down over there!

The Manager indicates the pouffe

George But Mr Willey can ex——
Manager Sit!

The Manager raises the stick and George sits. The Manager warily unlocks the bathroom door

   Edward comes out, very angrily

The Manager reacts to Edward in his underpants

Edward About time!

During the ensuing dialogue Edward storms into the bedroom, grabs his anorak, shoes and shirt and returns to the chair in the lounge where he left his trousers

Manager (*referring to Edward*) That's the young man from downstairs.
Edward (*stopping by George on his way to bedroom*) That's the second time you've locked me in!
Manager (*to Richard*) And that's the second person he's done it to, isn't it?
Richard Yes.

Manager (*to Edward who has returned with his clothes*) Did he make *you* take your clothes off, too?
Edward He bloody well did. (*He starts dressing*)

Pamela enters agitatedly and still very distraught. She stops on seeing Edward in the act of donning his trousers

Pamela Richard, what on earth's going on in here?
Richard Nothing, darling!

Richard emits his laugh. Everybody looks at him

Pamela (*coldly*) I see you're still here, George.
Manager Yes, madam and I wish . . . (*He stops*) You called him George!
Edward He likes to be called George.
Pamela (*to Edward, angrily*) I think the less you say, the better.
Edward Everybody seems to be against me today.
Pamela Are you surprised?
Edward Yes, I am. The only one I can understand being a bit narked is your husband.
Pamela Richard?
Edward But now he's got the queer tea boy he should be satisfied.
Pamela What?!

Richard and George look sick. Richard looks up to heaven. George buries his head in his hands

Manager What queer tea boy?
Pamela (*to Edward*) How dare you try to implicate my Richard in your love-life.
Richard Hear-hear.
Edward My love-life?
Pamela (*to Edward*) And, believe me, I have no objection to your being gay.
Edward (*to the Manager*) I ask you, do I look gay?
Manager Well, quite cheerful anyway.

Everybody looks sick

The Waiter enters with the trolley on which is laid out afternoon tea with several teapots, coffee pots, milk jugs, sugar bowls and a dozen cups and saucers. Jennifer is still on the lower shelf concealed by the table-cloth. He leaves the door open

Richard throws up his hands in despair

Waiter (*finally*) Tea for six-four-eight.
Manager (*glaring at him*) This is six-fifty.
Waiter I know that. Nobody in 648—so I think—where everybody? Answer—650.
Richard Thank you, Charlie Chan!
Waiter And to avoid error—three pot tea as well as three pot coffee.
Manager (*dismissing him*) That's enough, thank you.
Waiter Hope so. Plenty there for Mr Mrs Willey, Dr Mrs Christmas, Sir

Lady Easter, Ted, Charlie, Dickie, George and Noel. Eleven people. English cricket team, yes?

Manager Thank you!

Waiter (*moving to Edward, brightly*) You new here?

Edward Yes!

Waiter You lucky me bring twelve cups. Who sign?

Richard I'll sign.

Waiter (*very pleased*) Very good! Three pot tea, three pot coffee, three star brandy, thirty-three pounds.

Richard glares at the Waiter as he snatches the bill from him and signs

Thank you, *Sir Charlie*.

Richard (*quickly*) Richard Willey.

The Waiter realizes he is on to a good thing

Waiter (*to Richard*) Oh! You no more play pouf-pouf with Noel. (*He indicates George*)

George buries his head in anguish. Richard only just manages to refrain from throttling the Waiter

Manager (*to Richard*) Play pouf-pouf with Noel?

Pamela (*to the Waiter, tearfully angry*) How dare you say that about my husband. None of this would have happened if *he* (*she indicates* Edward) hadn't caught *you* cuddling *him*. (*She indicates George*)

The Waiter leaps into a kung-fu pose

Waiter }
Manager } (*together*) { Cuddling?!
                              { What?!

Edward Me?

Richard (*to Pamela*) Don't upset yourself again, darling.

Pamela (*hysterically*) It's bad enough George being queer without being told you're queer, too.

Richard (*trying to pacify her*) It's all right!

Pamela (*more hysterically*) The Home Office, the Foreign Office! How many more of you are there?!

Waiter Charlie, Teddy, Dickie, Georgie, Noel . . .

Pamela wails and runs out into the corridor

There is a pause as everybody turns to watch Pamela run off

Edward (*turning back*) Is any of this to do with *A Bit of the Other*?

They all slowly look around

Waiter (*to Edward*) You pouf-pouf?

Edward No, I'm not!

Waiter Oh, *Mrs Christmas* your friend, yes?

Richard No!

Waiter (*to Richard*) Me get confused.

Richard You'll get concussed. (*To the Manager*) Will you be mother?

The Manager glares but proceeds to pour the tea

(*Pulling the Waiter aside*) Just go away!
Waiter Talk too much, yes?
Richard Yes.
Waiter Must stop, yes?
Richard Yes.
Waiter OK. Tippee. (*He holds out his hand*)
Richard You've had enough tippee!
Waiter Oh, no, never enough tippee.
Richard Yes!
Waiter No. You like cakes with tea?

He lifts up the table-cloth which is draped over the trolley and Jennifer is there—still stuck. Only Richard and George see her. She gives a forlorn smile. Richard quickly checks that the Manager, who is pouring tea, has not noticed Jennifer

Richard No cakes!

Richard pulls down the cloth and covers Jennifer as the Manager appears beside Richard and George with tea

No. Never touch them, do we, Doctor?
George No. Never touch them. Bad for the figure, squashy tarts.

The Manager offers tea to Edward

Waiter Good-afternoon. (*He holds out his hand, surreptitiously, for a tip*)
Richard Good-afternoon. (*He gives him £20*)
Waiter Have a nice day. (*He holds out his hand again*)
Richard You, too. (*He gives him another £20*)
Waiter And please to offer cakes to all friends who not here—Ted, Charlie, Mrs Christmas, Lady Easter . . .

Richard hands over his wallet

Manager (*to the Waiter*) Thank you. You can retire now.
Richard He can certainly afford to.

Lily comes into 650 lounge from the corridor

Lily Sorry to intrude. (*To the Waiter*) I have been ringing room service for ages. Chatterton, six-four-nine.
Waiter So sorry, six-four-eight, six-fifty full-time job.

The Waiter exits into the corridor, leaving the door open

Lily (*seeing Edward*) Oh, how do you do.
Edward (*tersely*) How do you do, the name's Ted and I'm not.
Lily (*to the Manager*) I am trying to get a pot of tea.
Richard (*indicating the Manager*) Mother's in charge.
Manager Mother!

The Manager bangs the teapot down on the trolley. Jennifer's legs shoot out from the end of the trolley

Jennifer Ahhhhhh!

Everybody reacts

Manager (*staggered*) Who on earth is that?
George (*quickly*) Excuse me.

George grabs Jennifer's feet and runs towards the corridor pushing the trolley like a wheelbarrow. He half-stops and turns

(*Singing*) "This is the age of the train!"

George exits into the corridor with the trolley

Manager (*almost crying*) What the devil's he doing now?
Richard Playing pouf-pouf trains.

The Manger himself is now cracking up

Manager (*weeping*) I want no pouf-pouf trains in my hotel, do you hear? No pouf-pouf trains! I'll see you all downstairs in my signal box!

The Manager exits hysterically, leaving the door open

Edward (*dumbfounded*) Who the hell was that girl under the trolley?
Richard The floor waitress.
Lily No, no—I'm sure it was Mrs Bristow.
Edward Mrs Bristow?
Lily Yes. Sweet little thing. Works for the Prime Minister.
Edward What?!
Richard Thank you, Lily!
Edward Wait a minute. What's my wife doing on a trolley in the *Westminster Hotel*?
Richard Dr Christmas deals with all trick questions.

George enters still pushing trolley by the girl's ankles, Maria's this time, not Jennifer's

George I'm sorry, Mr Willey, there's no way out.
Richard Mr Pigden, please! Mrs Chatterton is not interested in our hotel arrangements.
Lily Mrs Chatterton is certainly interested in why you're calling Dr Christmas Mr Pigden.
Edward He likes to be called all sorts of funny names.
Lily Does he now?
Edward (*tapping the trolley with his stick*) Come on. Let's have you!

From under the trolley comes a loud but muffled "Ah". George goes to lift table-cloth

George Right!
Richard Pigden, please!

George I have nothing to hide. (*He goes to lift the table-cloth*)
Richard Pigden, please!
Lily Get Mrs Bristow out of there.
George (*with feigned surprise*) Mrs Bristow?
Lily
Edward } (*together*)   Mrs Bristow.
George This isn't Mrs Bristow.
Lily Who is it then?
George Maria, the chambermaid.
Lily Maria?
Edward The chambermaid?

George starts to remove the girl from the trolley

Richard Pigden, please!!

George produces Maria like a conjuror producing a rabbit from a hat

Maria (*with a flourish*) Riba, riba!
Richard Pigden, thank you!

Richard embraces George as Maria stands there arms aloft in a pose, beaming. Edward and Lily look for Jennifer under the trolley

Lily Where's Mrs Bristow?
George (*innocently*) Mrs Who?
Edward (*to Maria*) What happened to my wife?
Maria (*innocently*) Wife?
Lily The lady who's been running around up here.
George That was no lady, that was my chambermaid.
Maria Si. Being naughty naughty with Georgio. (*Dramatically*) Oh please do not report me to the manager. Maria have family to support in Barcelona. Mother, Father, brothers, sisters, little babies——
George (*interrupting*) All right, all right!
Lily (*to Richard*) You must think I'm a perfect idiot.
Richard Nobody's perfect, Lily.

Pamela enters 650 lounge from corridor. She is furious

Hello, darling! Are you all right now?
Pamela (*almost crying with anger*) No, I'm damn well not! I know what you've been doing this afternoon.
Richard (*on his dignity*) I've been doing my best to extricate Mr Pigden from his involvement with Ted and Maria.
Pamela And what about that woman?
Richard What woman?
Pamela The one in the red wig?
Richard Red wig?
Pamela The one I saw George remove from a tea trolley just now.

There is a fractional pause

Richard That was your mother, wasn't it, George?

Pamela It was Mrs Bristow!
Lily (*victorious*) I thought so.
Edward (*furious*) Right!
Richard Mrs who?
Pamela (*furiously pressing on*) One of the Prime Minister's secretaries! I've
seen her at Downing Street a dozen times.

Richard turns to George

Richard (*sternly*) What have you got to say for yourself, Pigden?
Pamela She wasn't seeing *George*, she was seeing *you*!
Richard Me! It was George who was smuggling her down the back stairs.
Pamela Yes, for *you*!
Richard (*to George*) Tell Pamela how you spent the afternoon in here with
Mrs Bristow.
Pamela (*furiously shouting*) It's no use, Richard, I know where George
spent this afternoon!
Richard Where?

*Pamela opens her mouth to speak but realizes and stops. For a moment time
stands still. Then George turns to the audience and gives his foolish laugh*

George I think this is the end.

Black-out

CURTAIN

FURNITURE AND PROPERTY LIST

ACT I

The Hotel Reception Area (Ground plan A)

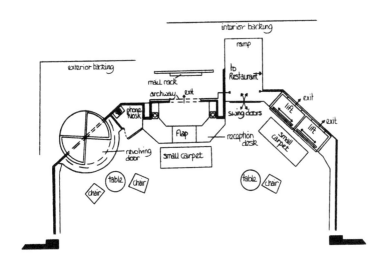

On stage: 2 small carpets
2 circular tables. *On* DR *table:* magazine (for **Pamela**)
3 chairs
Built-in reception desk with flap. *Above it:* RECEPTION DESK sign.
  Behind it: 2 boards for room keys with selection of keys including 650
  and 648, letter rack. *On it:* pen and stand, internal phone, reception bell
  (practical), hotel register, copy of *Daily Telegraph*
Dressing for restaurant backing
RESTAURANT and LIFT signs above entrances
Phone kiosk with phone and coinbox

Off stage: Silver tray containing 3 pots of coffee, 6 coffee cups and saucers, 3 milk
  jugs **(Waiter)**
Silver tray containing 6 sugar bowls **(Waiter)**
Mail **(Manager)**

Personal: **Richard:** wristwatch (used throughout), handkerchief, piece of paper with phone number
Pamela: wristwatch (used throughout), handbag containing 648 key and theatre ticket in envelope
George: wristwatch, spectacles (used throughout), briefcase with initials GP containing folder and papers, rolled umbrella, bowler hat
Manager: notebook, pen, wristwatch (used throughout)
Lily: handbag, wristwatch (used throughout)
Waiter: bill pad, pen (used throughout)

THE LOUNGES OF SUITES 648 AND 650 (GROUND PLAN B)

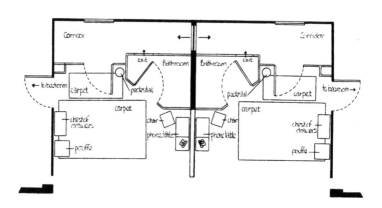

For set change on page 22

On stage: IN 648 LOUNGE
              Large carpet
              Small carpet
              Pouffe
              Phone table. *On it:* phone, directories, hotel information sheet
              Chair
              Chest of drawers
              Pedestal with vase of flowers
              DO NOT DISTURB sign on corridor door handle

              IN 650 LOUNGE
              Large carpet
              Small carpet
              Pouffe
              Phone table. *On it:* phone, directories, hotel information sheet
              Chair
              Chest of drawers
              Pedestal with vase of flowers

Off stage: Trolley. *On it:* towels, dusters, polish etc. **(Maria)**
              Dirty towels **(Maria)**

Trolley. *On top shelf:* large table-cloth, ice-bucket containing bottle of
champagne, 2 champagne glasses, plate of sandwiches **(Waiter)**
Richard's pyjamas, slippers, dressing-gown **(George)**
Bottle of "Benzedrine" pills **(George)**
Glass of champagne **(Richard)**
Glass scent-spray **(Pamela)**
Glass of water **(Richard)**
Trolley. *On it:* ice-bucket containing bottle of champagne, 2 champagne
glasses, oysters **(Waiter)**
Bottle of "hay fever" pills **(George)**
Towel **(Richard)**

Personal: **Maria:** notepad
George: briefcase, 650 door key
Richard: 648 door key, handkerchief, wallet containing £20 and £10 notes
Waiter: pass key
Jennifer: outrageous "feminine" sunglasses, red wig
Manager: set of pass keys

THE LOUNGE AND BEDROOM OF SUITE 648 (GROUND PLAN C)

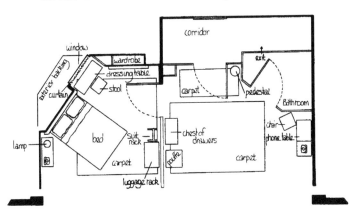

For set change on page 44

On stage: IN 648 LOUNGE
As before

IN 648 BEDROOM
Carpet
Curtains at window
Fitted wardrobe. *In it:* clothes, including **Pamela**'s
Dressing-table
Stool
Small double bed with bedclothes. *On it:* **Pamela**'s négligé, magazine
Bedside table. *On it:* table lamp, phone
Suitcase rack. *On it:* suitcase
Dumb valet

ACT II

THE LOUNGE AND BEDROOM OF SUITE 648

On stage: As before

Personal: **Richard:** red wig and **Jennifer**'s sunglasses in dressing-gown pockets

THE LOUNGES OF SUITES 648 AND 650

For set change on page 48

On stage: As before

Off stage: Glass of champagne **(Jennifer)**

Personal: **George:** briefcase
Richard: Pamela's sunglasses
Lily: handbag

THE HOTEL RECEPTION AREA

For set change on page 58

Strike: Circular table DR and 2 chairs

Set: Papers (for **Manager**) on reception desk

Off stage: Silver tray containing trick glass of brandy **(Waiter)**

Personal: **Lily:** handbag
George: briefcase, money clip containing £20 and £10 notes, coin in pocket
Edward: walking stick, bandaged foot, addressed envelope containing note on *Westminster Hotel* paper
Jennifer: red wig and sunglasses

THE LOUNGE AND BEDROOM OF SUITE 648

For set change on page 62

Set: Ice bucket containing bottle of champagne on bedside table
2 glasses of champagne (for **Richard** and **Pamela**)
Richard's blazer, shirt and trousers in wardrobe
Richard's shoes by bed

THE LOUNGE AND BEDROOM OF SUITE 650 (GROUND PLAN D)

For set change on page 66

Set: IN 650 LOUNGE
Jennifer's wig and sunglasses on chair
George's briefcase by phone table

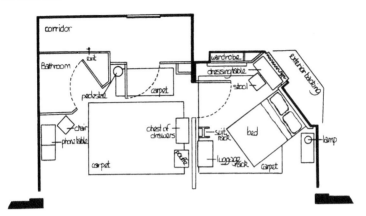

On stage: IN 650 BEDROOM
          Carpet
          Curtains at window
          Fitted wardrobe
          Dressing-table
          Stool
          Small double bed with bedclothes
          Bedside table. *On it:* table lamp, phone
          Suitcase rack
          Dumb valet
          Trolley. *On top shelf:* large table-cloth, ice-bucket containing bottle of
            champagne, plate of sandwiches
          Key in bedroom door (practical)

Personal: **Richard:** wallet containing £20 and £10 notes
          Lily: handbag
          Manager: set of pass keys

THE LOUNGES OF SUITES 648 AND 650

For set change on page 72

On stage: As before

Off stage: Trolley. *On top shelf:* large table-cloth, ice-bucket containing bottle of
            champagne, plate of sandwiches **(Jennifer)**

Personal: **Edward:** walking stick, bandaged foot
          George: 650 bedroom key in pocket

THE LOUNGE AND BEDROOM OF SUITE 650

For set change on page 77

Set: **Edward's** shoes, anorak, trousers, shirt, walking stick on suitcase rack

Off stage: Trolley. *On top shelf:* large table-cloth, 3 teapots containing tea, 3 coffee
pots, milk jugs, sugar bowls, 6 teacups and saucers, 6 coffee cups and
saucers, bottle of brandy, brandy glasses **(Waiter)**

Personal: **Richard:** wallet containing £20 notes
Lily: handbag

LIGHTING PLOT

Property fittings required: nil

Various interior settings

ACT I

To open: Full general lighting

No cues

ACT II

To open: Full general lighting

Cue 1   **George:** "I think this is the end."   (Page 88)

        Black-out

EFFECTS PLOT

ACT I

Cue 1   **Richard** and the **Manager** are transfixed
           Music, fade when set in position

Cue 2   **George** moves to go   (Page 23)
           650 lounge phone rings

Cue 3   **Waiter:** "Sign, please."   (Page 27)
           650 lounge phone rings

Cue 4   **George** comes out of the bathroom with **Richard**'s clothes (Page 29)
           648 lounge phone rings

ACT II

Cue 5   **George:** "... his wife is my boyfriend."   (Page 49)
           650 lounge phone rings

Cue 6   **Edward:** "Or television or film work."   (Page 61)
           Internal phone rings

Cue 7   **Richard:** "—no distractions—relaxed!"   (Page 63)
           648 bedroom phone rings

Cue 8   **George** pushes the trolley back into the bathroom   (Page 65)
           *Loud crash of glass, china etc., then general smashing and
           breaking noises*

Cue 9   **Edward:** "It all sounds very interesting."   (Page 75)
           Loud glass crash

MADE AND PRINTED IN GREAT BRITAIN BY
LATIMER TREND & COMPANY LTD, PLYMOUTH
MADE IN ENGLAND

Ingram Content Group UK Ltd.
Milton Keynes UK
UKHW022207120323
418425UK00014B/205

9 780573 016073